Ellen Johnson

across the river

iUniverse, Inc.
Bloomington

across the river

iUniverse books may be ordered through booksellers or by contacting:

iUniverse
1663 Liberty Drive
Bloomington, IN 47403
www.iuniverse.com
1-800-Authors (1-800-288-4677)

ISBN: 978-1-4620-3012-5 (sc)
ISBN: 978-1-4620-3013-2 (ebook)
ISBN: 978-1-4620-3014-9 (dj)

Printed in the United States of America

iUniverse rev. date: 6/22/2011

introduction

This book is dedicated to my beloved mother, Ann Reynalds. She has not only been an inspiration to her children but a remarkably loving, caring, wise, and extraordinary human being. She was a pillar of strength through the good times and the bad. Even though she had the opportunity to experience her mother's love for only a short period of time, she didn't deprive her children of her love and affection. She instilled in us tough love. She raised us to always believe in God, to keep the faith, and to never give up on our dreams. She inspired us to believe in ourselves and to have self-discipline, self-control, patience, courage, determination, and perseverance. She taught us to always ask God for strength—just as she did, to keep her family together.

One of her mottos was "there are no shortcuts in life." We have to work hard to reach our goals, overcoming obstacles and stumbling blocks along the way, never giving up and always keeping the faith. She inspired us to be courteous and to have dignity and integrity in whatever we do. She gave us the love, security, and stability that every child needs and deserves. She wanted us to appreciate the necessary things in life instead of materialistic things. Mom will always be remembered as an astonishing woman who motivated her children to pursue their dreams and create a better future.

I humbly ask each and every one of my readers, regardless of how near or far you are, or how rich or poor you are, please reach out to your mom. Remind her how much you love her. No matter how busy you are, please find the time to do so. She probably wants you to reach out to her and to hear your voice. Like all of us, she needs to feel loved and appreciated. Spend quality time with her. Whatever difference you may have with your mom, throw it aside. She carried you under her heart for nine months; when her heart beat, so did yours. Being a mother is a tough job. I strongly urge you to find it within your heart to reach out to your mom. Please do not let anything or anyone come between that relationship. Life is precious and short. You never know when it will be her last day on earth. Let your words to her be positive and sincere at all times, so that they can linger deep within her soul. You may never know when her words to you will be the last. Always remember that nothing—and I mean nothing—can take away a mother's love for her child. She needs your unconditional love to help make her life worth living. As children, we can never finish repaying our mother for all she has done for us. Our mom has a lot to do with who we are today, and a mother's work is never done where her children are concerned.

If your mom gave you to your grandmother or any other relative to raise you, or you have been adopted, it's not because she didn't love you. It's because she wanted the best for you. She wanted someone to take very good care of you. It must have been the hardest thing she ever had to do. Please, don't ever hate your mom; forgive her for whatever wrong you think she may have done to you.

chapter 1

My mother came from a biracial family. Her mother, Julie, was a beautiful black woman, a seamstress from the sunny Caribbean, the spice island of Grenada. Her father, Bert, was an agriculturist, the son of a judge from Great Britain. Her parents had to sneak and hide in order to see each other. Their forbidden love and marriage was in trouble from the start.

My mother was the only girl in a family of three children, and her parents' relationship faced discrimination and racism. Her dad would leave in the wee hours of the morning from the countryside of Saunters to go to the city of St. Georges for his job. He was unaware of the verbal, emotional, and psychological abuse his wife and children were suffering at the hands of his family. They were called racial slurs all the time. In those days, racial discrimination was widespread.

Her mother, Julie, could no longer stand the abuse. One day, she packed up, left her children behind, and moved to Venezuela. Upon their return from school, my mom (at the tender age of nine years old) and her siblings, David and Herbert, learned of their mother's departure. They were heartbroken, especially my mom; she was devastated. She loved her mother dearly. Her father, Bert, provided financially and emotionally for his children. He showed them love and affection but still could not replace their mother's love. Bert turned a blind eye to the fact that his children were being abused at the hands of his family, whom he entrusted them to while he was away from home. They could not complain, or the situation would get worse for them.

Her father had a beautiful farm that included horses, fowls, and pigs. He would pay the workers to feed and care for the animals and even train the horses. After Bert left for work at 5:00 a.m., my mother's aunt would wake up my mom and her brothers and then make them carry heavy buckets of hog food on their heads up a steep hill to feed the hogs—instead of having the workers do it, who were being paid to do their job. The workers that were hired to care for the animals were eventually laid off, unknown to Bert. My mother's aunts pocketed the money and had Mom doing all the chores instead. My mother had to grow up the fast way. She had to help take care of the horses and feed the other animals, but my mother took a negative situation and turned it around for herself and her siblings. The way she saw it, she got the opportunity to learn to ride the horses.

Mom continued to grieve for her mother, taking comfort in time spent with Angel, the horse she considered her best friend. Her father taught her and her brothers to defend themselves in times of trouble. Mom said that Grandpa would tell her, "You are my only girl child, and I don't want you to grow up to be a damn fool for others to take advantage of, because your mother's not around." She said that on more than one occasion, she almost got raped while running errands for her Aunt Jaclyn. She was able to kick the pedophile in his groin, and with the help of Angel, they galloped away as fast as they could until they got home safely. Her education was put on hold while she continued to help care for the animals. Her brothers, however, were not denied their education.

Her mother, Julie, assumed she had made the right decision by leaving her children in the care of their father and his family. Mom was unaware of the letters and gifts her mom sent to her and her brothers; they were never given to them. They were either sent back to her mother in Venezuela or were hidden. Grandpa was over six feet tall. His good looks, charm, and personality had the women falling at his feet. There wasn't much time for him to have a family life. Nevertheless, he always found time to be part of his children's lives. He also had seven other children by different women.

At the age of twenty-one, Mom got engaged. Even though wedding plans were in motion, she and her fiancé, Bill, met with opposition from both sides of the family. They had no choice but to end their relationship. Although she was an adult, if she had gone through with the wedding, her family would have disowned her. She chose to have her love child alone and was heartbroken over the breakup of the relationship of her first love. She was forbidden to see her ex-fiancé, but one day, Bill decided to pay an unexpected visit to Mom and their daughter (who is my oldest sibling). He was greeted by three German shepherds waiting for him. Armed with presents, he had to scale a high wall to get away alive. Whenever he tried to send anything to his child, Mom's family would send the packages back to him.

Her friends decided to step in by bringing the items from Bill to Mom and the baby, which included baby formula, love letters, pictures, and more, hoping they would not be discovered. Her family became very suspicious of the friends' frequent visits and the loud laughter coming from Mom's room. One rainy night when the aunts knew Mom was asleep, they went into her room and searched from top to bottom. Mom was not much of a heavy sleeper, except when it rained heavily. Her aunts were aware of that and seized the opportunity to search her room. Snooping around, they finally found the items Bill had been sending to her and the baby. They were taken away or destroyed. Her friends were forbidden from visiting Mom and her daughter at home; they could only see each other at church. Even then, they were kept under a watchful eye. Mom once said to me that her aunts took away her happiness because "they didn't want to lose their slave."

Mom went on to become a nurse's aide. She didn't socialize; after work, she would return home to continue to care for her daughter. She was not allowed to have any visitors at her aunt's home.

Five years later, Mom met and fell in love with a dashing middle-aged man named Harris, twenty-five years her senior. He was known as a ladies' man, and he captured Mom's heart. His business, meanwhile, was heading for bankruptcy. After a whirlwind romance, she and her daughter, Mindy, moved in with Harris. They had a beautiful home overlooking the ocean. Five years later, she had another beautiful daughter named Cindy. My mom had the golden touch when it came to business; her husband's business began to flourish. Customers were coming in from every part of the city to their store, which was located in the countryside. Both children had a nanny to care for them while their parents worked. The customers were happy with the service they were getting, and they could get items there that they couldn't get in the city. If Mom and Harris didn't have something in stock; they ordered it to satisfy their customers. Mom seemed to be very happy. She had everything going for her—a career, a loving husband, and two healthy, beautiful children. Beside the nannies, she also had two gardeners and a butler.

My mom worked long hours at the store, making sure the customers' needs were met. While they waited on their orders, they would have their vehicles tuned up; she was also a mechanic. She was a beautiful woman with bluish-green eyes, who was not afraid to get her hands dirty in oil. She worked hard at having a successful business, a career, and a happy home. Even though her children had nannies, she always tried her best to spend as much time as possible with them. She never took anything in life for granted. She always said to her children, "One minute you can be at top of the world, and in the split of a second, it can all come crashing down on you." She taught her children to never look down or turn up their noses at anyone less fortunate than them, including the homeless. She said, "Offer them a hot meal if you can, because you never know what circumstances in life may have led them into that situation. Always be humble and courteous. Do not let success go to your head, because the same people you meet on our way up are the ones you'll meet on your way back down, especially when the tables are turned against you."

One bright sunny day, her best friend, Marsha, whom she had not seen in quite a while, paid her an unexpected visit. She confided in Mom that she was pregnant and that her parents had put her out. She had nowhere to go. She asked Mom if she could stay with her for a while, until she had the baby. Mom told her she would have to discuss it with her common-law husband. Being the kindhearted person Mom was, she persuaded her husband, who had a cold personality, to help her friend. He finally agreed to allow Marsha to move in with them. Shortly thereafter, Marsha moved in.

Soon, Mom became suspicious of Marsha's behavior. On one particular day, the customers were coming and going, waiting for their cars and their order of supplies. She was alone at the shop, trying to handle everything by herself. Some of the customers were getting impatient, and Harris was nowhere to be seen. Mom had one of the workers take over the store while she went in search of him. Nothing had prepared her for what she encountered. She found her husband and best friend in the master bedroom in a compromising position. She felt numb. Shocked at what she had just seen, she calmly closed the door behind her, walked back down stairs to the store, and handled her business in a professional manner.

The mechanic shop was open at all hours in order to accommodate their friends and customers. Mom never got much sleep; she was constantly on the go, trying her best to keep the customers happy and satisfied. Her relationship with her husband went sour. Her so-called best friend was now in charge of the household, giving orders to the workers. Meanwhile, her husband acted like he was the victim. Mom moved into the guest room with her children until she could make other arrangements. She finally took her children and moved in with her grandmother, who had previously rescued her from the cruel hands of her aunts. Mom's husband was an influential member of society. When he was heading for bankruptcy, his so-called friends suddenly disappeared, taking items on credit and skipping out of town; they were nowhere to be seen or found. Now that he was successful and on top of the world, they were all back in his life.

Men were looked up to as the dominant head of the house, and women were supposed to stay at home, take care of the children, and do the household chores. Mom was not allowed to withdraw any money from their joint account. Everything was frozen. Her world was closing in on her. She was a humble person, knowing how far she had come from. She showed compassion to her friend when need of help, and both Marsha and Harris took her kindness for weakness. Harris's influential friends kept tabs on her every move. He made her life unbearable. Mom had put aside some money for a rainy day. The workers, whom she always treated with respect and dignity, came to her rescue, but then she suffered yet another emotional blow. To add insult to injury, she found out on her return from work that Harris had kidnapped Cindy, the child they had together, and had put the house in her name. Back then, there were no strict laws to protect children and women. They had to fend for themselves. She was emotionally crushed. With her husband's money and power, she did not stand much of a chance of winning. He wanted to bring her to her knees, and he did. Mom didn't allow her pride to stand in the way; she stooped to her husband's every demand, yet he refused to let her see their child. She became an emotional wreck. At the time, she was one of the few female mechanics in the country who could drive a racecar. She got respect and recognition from members of the community. Being a strong, beautiful, independent woman, he needed to have control over her. He didn't care how he did it, whom he hurt in the process, or how many lives were destroyed.

Her father and brothers had moved to another country, but they continued to communicate. Mom later joined her father, Bert, in Trinidad, to start all over again. Her grief from having to flee from her country in fear and shame, leaving both her children behind, was incomprehensible. Grandpa felt her pain. His warm embraces and kind words helped her tremendously. He helped build her self-esteem back up, and slowly, her heart and soul began to heal. She found a job as a nurse's aide and started saving money to send to her oldest child, Mindy. She became closer to the wonderful teachings and the word of God. It helped fill the void deep within her heart.

Several years later, Dad met Mom, but she was not interested in him or any other man. He continued to pursue her. He told me later on that he had a very difficult time talking to her, much less taking her out on a date. She admitted that she saw him in her dreams and was told that he was the one to be her husband. One of the things we learned was that when Mom said she had a dream, depending on what she dreamt, it would come true. She was right on the money with her dreams. This made us cautious, especially whenever she warned us to be careful of our surroundings.

Dad was much older than Mom. He was a successful realtor and the only son from a family of three. Dad finally professed his love to her, but there were obstacles that stood in their way. His sisters were aware of her children from previous relationships and what had transpired in her life. His sisters, Kara and Melinda, used the information to their advantage, calling her awful names. Grandpa was always there to give her the emotional support she needed.

Dad had his sisters and their children educated in Europe. Even though they had a family of their own, they felt threatened by any woman that came into his life. They were not going to let anyone stand in their way. All they had to do was ask him for what they wanted financially, and they would get it. He would yield to their demands and spoil them. He later told me that being the oldest, he felt he had an obligation to take care of his sisters. Before their mother died, he promised her that he would take care of them. They took advantage of the situation.

Dad and Mom had three beautiful children: Lenny, Mitch, and Ellen. They eventually got married. She finally sent for her oldest child, Mindy, but still could not have any contact with her second child, Cindy. Her letters and gifts were returned unopened, and her heart continued to ache.

History soon began repeating itself. Dad had lived his life as a bachelor for so long—being carefree yet cautious in life—that when he finally met the woman of his dreams, as he later said, he didn't know how to be responsible in that department. He left everything up to Mom. When we were small, Dad moved to Curacao to study dentistry, promising to send for Mom as soon as he settled down. As time went by, his letters became few. Financially, things were not going right for her again. Prior to leaving, he left his nephew Carter in charge of his properties. Even though he left instructions about how much money should be given to Mom every month, his nephew never gave her a cent or went by to check on her and the children. Being the classy lady Mom was, she never made a scene or demanded that Carter give her what was due to her. She left it alone and suffered in silence. Dad later said he did everything legally to ensure his nephew took care of Mom financially. When he checked with his nephew, he would tell him everything was fine with Mom and the children. It was like Mom thought she deserved what was happening to her. Since her mom left her at an early age, and her so-called best friend and husband played her as a fiddle, it was okay for everyone to step on her toes; she didn't complained. Mom didn't give up though; she continued praying, asking God for his strength and guidance.

Dad finally sent for Mom to continue her studies in nursing. Before leaving, Mom left us in the responsible care of a family member. They both were working and studying. They continued to communicate and contributed financially toward the well-being of their children. In the midst of her studies, Mom received word from another family member, insisting that if Mom wanted to see us alive, she should return home. Upon hearing the news, she immediately dropped everything, including her studies, her job, and of course Dad, and returned to Trinidad. She was overwhelmed by the appearance of her children, who were healthy when she left them. Without delay, she took us for a physical examination. Lenny and I were malnourished. Needless to say, the pediatrician said I also had an ear infection due to "the raising up by one hand." I was also hard of hearing. Mom was devastated. Her top priority was to be with her children. As a responsible parent, she devoted her time and energy to ensure her children received the best medical care. Dad remained in Curacao to continue his education. He promised to be there for us emotionally and financially. However, as time went by, he kept in touch less and less. Once again, Mom stood alone with God's loving arms around her, along with the love and emotional support of Grandpa and Uncle Bert Jr.

Grandpa helped move her to Maraval in Port of Spain, where she would be close to the nearest and best hospital. Grandpa bought Mom a big house across the river, leading into the reservoir. At the back of the house was a ravine, with spring water coming in from the mountain. Mom was about to be faced with the most challenging experience of her life.

Mom seldom took time to relax. Her house was the only one across the river, and it was surrounded by several parcels of land. Being the only house across the river, the government officials said that they could only supply her with electrical power if there was more than one house located there. Grandpa, being an agriculturist, knew how to survive. He showed Mom how to use an oil lamp and agricultural tools and how to plant vegetables to survive.

We all had to attend Sunday mass regularly. Mom always made sure we were clean and dressed us conservatively. At an early age, Mom taught us how to pray and how to sit and keep our posture straight, without resting our elbows at the table. She even showed us the correct way to use a knife and fork, and how to place a napkin on our lap. Table manners were very important to Mom. She taught us how to write the capital and common letters of the alphabet by holding our hand, guiding us every step of the way until we got it right. Mom taught us how to read the clock by letting us know how many seconds make a minute, and how many minutes make an hour. She made sure we had a watch to wear at an early age. Mom didn't wait for the teachers to teach us everything. She had the patience to teach us what we needed to know. When we started kindergarten, we already knew the alphabet and how to read the clock. She instilled in her children how to show love, by kissing each other before leaving and when returning home. One of the things I always admired about Mom was that whenever we talked about tomorrow, she wanted us to say at all times, "Tomorrow, please God," or "God willing." She always reminded us that "tomorrow is not ours." There are no guarantees in life. When we fall asleep, there's no guarantee we'll wake up the following day.

The elementary school we attended was not far from home. Lenny continued to attend the same school with me, except when he was hospitalized. He had a teacher who would go to the hospital to teach him. Whenever Lenny was at home, he didn't play outside much. If he was not reading or doing homework, he was drawing a picture of Jesus or the chalice. Lenny drew magnificent pictures that we all admired. His work looked professional. Mom saved his drawings and other important things, including my long hair that was cut when I was seven, and placed them in a special trunk. Lenny wanted to become a priest, and I wanted to be a nun. The neighbors were very impressed with his drawings and paintings. They offered to pay for his work, but Mom wouldn't take a dime; instead she would offer them for free. This was part of Mom's kindness.

It was during one of those days, while Lenny was coloring a picture of the chalice, he suddenly raised his head up and told Mom that her cousin Olivia would be coming home shortly and would be very hungry. Mom asked him what she should do. He told her to cook Olivia's favorite meal of cornmeal and fish. At first, I thought he was kidding. I remembered laughing because I found it amusing. A short time later, I could not believe my ears when I heard Olivia calling out from across the river. She needed Mom to put away Rover, our dog. Boy was she hungry. She had returned from the beach and was heading home when she decided to stop by. She was surprised that Mom had already prepared her favorite dish. She wanted to know how Mom knew she was coming and what she wanted to eat. Mom told her what Lenny had said. He was also her Godson. Olivia teased Lenny, "I've got to watch you; you're minding my business!" Lenny just smiled.

I began paying close attention to him, especially when he said something out of the ordinary. One day, I asked Mom, "How does he know those things?" Mom said it was a gift from God. She went on to explain that when she was pregnant with him, it was the first time she read the Bible often. Mom made sure we made our First Communion and were confirmed. She did a terrific job making sure we attended Sunday school after morning mass. We had to learn the Ten Commandments, read the Bible, and pass quizzes on a regular basis. Mom made sure we did everything by the book, following the instructions. I can still remember the Sunday morning Lenny and Mitch were dressed in their white long-sleeve shirts, black pants, and ties. I was in a white dress and veil. It was a sacred day in our lives. As we walked up the aisle to the altar, Father Michael lectured about the steps we were about to take and how we now needed to keep God first in everything we did. Mom and Mindy sat among the other parents, admiring how handsome and beautiful her children looked. It was a solemn occasion without Dad at her side. With tears streaming down her cheeks, she tried to put on a brave and happy face, but underneath it all, she looked so sad without Dad standing at her side for that special event.

chapter 2

Lenny was a special child of God. One day, Lenny and I were walking home from school when two boys got into a fight. One of the boys took off running, and the other one picked up a stone and threw it at the boy. Instead of hitting his target, it hit Lenny in his chest. The boy then took off running. One of the teachers who had seen what had happened came to assist Lenny. She sat him down on the steps in front of the church and asked one of the kids to get him some water. Lenny didn't say anything; he just kept holding his chest. She told us to stay there, and she went back upstairs and called for an ambulance.

Meanwhile, Mom was on her way up the hill to meet us after picking up Mitch from his school. When they arrived, she saw us sitting on the church steps. I told Mom what happened, and she just kept on saying, "Jesus, Mary, and Joseph." When the teacher finally came back downstairs, she met Mom. After explaining what she saw, we all waited for the ambulance. Lenny leaned his head on Mom's chest as she gently massaged his back. The teacher promised to file a report with the principal and the board of education. We all knew the young man who threw the stone. He didn't live too far from us. His father was a respectable person in the community, but the son had been back and forth through the court system. His mother was always sickly and couldn't do much. She left everything up to the husband in regards to controlling their son. The ambulance finally arrived, and the teacher promised Mom she would take Mitch and me home. When we arrived home, Rover alerted Mindy, who came to greet us from across the river. The teacher told her what had happened.

Mindy was taken aback. She sounded like Mom when she kept repeating, "No one can predict what can happen in the split of a second." Mindy wanted us to retire to bed early so we could get up in time for school, but I believed she didn't want us hearing any bad news. That night, Mom arrived home late from the hospital. I was awakened by the sound of Rover's barking. I jumped out of bed; I needed to know how Lenny was doing. Mindy tried to get me back to bed, but Mom understood my concern and allowed me to stay up for a few minutes. She gently told me that Lenny was admitted to the hospital for observation. The doctors had to take more tests to know the extent of his injury. Mom shielded us from knowing how serious Lenny's condition really was.

The following day, Carlos—the boy who threw the rock—came to inquire about Lenny's health. After learning he was admitted to the hospital, he sincerely apologized to Mom for his actions. Mom didn't forget to give him a stern lecture, which his parents were afraid of doing. He wanted to know what he could do to make up for the wrong he had done. Mom just wanted him to turn his life around, become a better person, and focus on his education. Lenny's teacher, Mr. Bernard, stopped by from time to time to find out how Lenny was doing. He spent a month at the hospital. He was later transferred to the San Fernando Hospital for further evaluation. His life was never the same. Carlos's father came by to offer his heartfelt apology for what his son did; Mom let him have it by giving him a stern lecture.

Shortly after Confirmation, both Lenny and I got sick. Mom took us to the doctor while Mindy took care of Mitch. At night, Mom would sleep with one of us in each arm to monitor us closely. She knew she had a tough road ahead of her to help keep Lenny alive. He had to be hospitalized on several occasions. Most times upon her return, Mom would be so exhausted from the long journey to and from the hospital, she would just collapse on the bed. It was heart-wrenching to see her like that. Mostly on Sundays, Mom would dress Mitch and me in our best outfits to visit Lenny, and he was always so happy to see us. Mom usually would have to get the nurse's permission to bring him ice cream or bananas from the garden. He enjoyed eating the bananas, telling Mom what a good farmer she was. When it was time to leave him, it was tough. Sometimes the nurses would give us extra time to spend with Lenny, knowing how far we had traveled to see him, which made it a little easier to part.

On one particular day, Mom took me with her to visit Lenny at the hospital. We were three years apart and missed each other dearly. Upon our arrival, Lenny was sitting on the bed drawing a picture of Jesus. He acknowledged Mom and me as he continued to draw the picture. Then he raised his head, and with a sad expression on his face, he told Mom he was going to die and that his final wish was to die at home. Shocked, Mom asked him how he knew he was going to die. He said he dreamt he was surrounded by angels and they were pulling him toward them. Mom asked how he knew they were angels, and he said, "Because they all had wings." Upon hearing this, Mom held me by the hand and told him she'd be right back. We left the room in search of the attending pediatrician.

As soon as the doctor saw Mom, he told her, "I'm sorry. We've done all we could to save Lenny's life, but I'm afraid he's not going to make it. He's going to die within a month." Mom asked the doctor if he had told Lenny of his fate, and he said that he hadn't. Mom told him that Lenny was aware he was going to die and wanted to be at home. The doctor angrily told her if she discharged him from the hospital, he was going to call the police and have her arrested. Mom said, "Go right ahead and call the police. I'm taking my child home for his final wish." I tugged at Mom's hand. I was scared that the police would take her away from us. I thought that we may never see her again. I asked her to called Uncle David and Cousin Alfonso, who was a superintendent of the police. Mom had stood alone for so long with God at her side, throughout her trials and tribulations, she thought she could continue to do it all by herself—until now. The pain was unbearable.

Feeling numb and reeling from shock, Mom made the call to both relatives. With me standing at her side, we returned to Lenny's room and waited. Mom sobbed uncontrollably. Lenny lovingly stroked her face, too weak to hold her head in his arms. He said to her, "Mama, everything is going to be all right. We are surrounded by angels; they are watching over us." His words seemed to have a strong impact on her, and she dried her tears. With a smile on her weary face, she tried to cheer him up the best way she knew how.

Cousin Alfonso finally arrived in his uniform. He was on duty and had taken his lunch break to be there for Mom in a time of emotional need. He was followed by Uncle David and Cousin Olivia. Mom held my hand tightly and headed for the nurse's station in search of Dr. Marshall. As soon as he saw Mom accompanied by the officer and her relatives, there was not much for him to say. After asking about Lenny's condition, Officer Alfonso told Dr. Marshall, "Lenny should not be denied his final wish, which is to die at home." Without any further argument, the necessary papers were drawn up and signed. Mom did it with a heavy heart. She carried her dying son in her arms, with his checkered colored pajamas on as he requested. Before leaving the hospital, he thanked the nurses for taking good care of him. Lenny told Mom he needed to see his best friend, Kenneth. They were both admitted to the hospital on the same day and were diagnosed with the same medical condition. They had been in and out of the hospital around the same time. Lenny told him not to be afraid, that they would meet in heaven soon. They warmly embraced each other, promising to meet on the other side. Lenny was loved by everyone who came in contact with him, including the doctors and nurses. They complimented Mom on what a special boy he was. He certainly was an extraordinary, gifted, blessed child; we all knew it. The parting was tough; the doctors and nurses, from the other wards came to say good-bye to him. They lined the corridor with flowers, hugs, kisses, and handshakes to cheer him on as Mom wearily carried her dying son home.

The drive home was solemn. Cousin Alfonso drove ahead, while Uncle David followed closely behind. Cousin Olivia sat in front, and I sat next to Mom in the back as she cradled Lenny's slim, long body in her loving arms. Throughout the long journey, Lenny slept peacefully in Mom's arms, and she silently wept. I leaned on my brother's arms, trying to hold on to him, never wanting to let him go. Mom was heartbroken; she later said that upon learning the news of her of son's fate, she felt emptiness sweep through her body, which she had never experienced before. She felt she could no longer go on without him, but she had to be strong for her other children.

During the drive home, Lenny woke up and told Mom he wanted to pick out his suit and the coffin to be buried in. Uncle David blew the horn for Uncle Alfonso to stop; then he explained what Lenny wanted to do. He called his superiors at the precinct to let them know he had a family emergency and that he would be in late. It was the most heartbreaking experience a mother and sister could ever experience. At the tailor shop, his measurements were taken. He chose a brown material to be made into a double-breasted suit. Upon learning of his fate, the tailor didn't charge Mom. The next stop was the funeral agency of his choice. Lenny chose a brown coffin, and then we made another stop for his shirt and tie. Mom was once again spared the expenses for the burial. The final stop was to see the priest. There were two of them staying at the rectory. He made his final choice.

Shortly after Lenny returned home, we learn from the death news on the radio that his best friend, Kenneth, from the hospital had died.

During Lenny's final time, he told Mom what he wanted to eat and drink. His favorite drink was made from sorrel, which Mom grew in the vegetable garden. She always made sure the sorrel was dried, boiled, sweetened, and ready to serve with ice, upon his request. He was a well-mannered young man. Even before he got ill, he was never disrespectful to Mom or anyone else. He showed me the true meaning of what being close to God meant—with his quiet thoughts, his beautiful smile, and his interpretation of the verses in the Bible. Lenny was always ahead of us in knowing the scriptures. Most times, he would preach the Word of God to us. With a smile on her face, Mom admired him for being so gifted. Most times we conversed, it seemed like I was talking to someone from beyond. He seemed much wiser than his age. I could not help wanting to spend as much time with him as possible when he described what heaven looked like. He seemed to be from the other side, passing through on earth for only a short time. He was destined to become a priest. His answers to Mom were always "Yes, thank you," or "No thank you, Ma." I never saw him get angry, even when I would take his shirts to wear. He would just smile and tell me if I wanted the shirts, I could have them. He would ask Mom if it was possible for him to have his favorite dish of eddoes, dasheen, or white yam with oak roes, which Mom also grew in the vegetable garden, with salt fish and cucumbers, tossed in olive oil. The rest of the family came from near and far to be there for Mom and to help cater to Lenny's every need. Even Father Michael would stop by from time to time to see how Lenny was doing or if Mom needed anything.

One night, in the wee hours of the morning, I was awakened by a loud scream coming from Mom's room. Without knocking, I rushed in, thinking someone was hurting her. As I entered the room, I could not believe my eyes. Mom's room was brightly lit with large white candles placed in saucers containing water. The room looked like heaven. Mom was sitting up in the bed, holding Lenny tightly in her arms, rocking him back and forth as he screamed and twisted in pain. Her eyes were closed. With tears streaming down her face, she was singing, "rock of ages, cleft for me, let me not hide thy self from thee." Suddenly, she opened her eyes, saw me standing in the middle of the room, and motioned for me to go back to my room. I was unable to move. I felt helpless and weak as I stood there staring at what was enfolding before me. I silently asked God to show me something in my sleep, to help ease Lenny's pain, and to help my heartbroken Mom get some sleep. As soon as Mom was through singing "Rock of Ages," Lenny pleaded with her, "Sing more hymns, Ma?" Sounding weak and weary, she sang "Just as I Am Without One Plea," followed by "Precious Lord, sweet hour of prayer, which calls me from a world of care, and bids me at my father's throne, make all my wants, and wishes known." Mom kept singing hymn after hymn. I felt my little heart breaking into many small pieces as I slowly walked back to my room and then crawled under the covers. I pleaded with God to answer my prayer. My brother was in excruciating pain, and there was nothing any one of us could do.

The following morning, when I awoke, Mom said to me, "Thank you, my child, for what you told me to do. It helped ease your brother's pain; he was able to get some sleep. As a matter of fact, he's still sleeping." Surprised, I asked my Mom what I had told her to do. She said, "You don't know what you did?" She explained that I got up from sleeping, sat on the bed, and called out for her to come. When she came, I told her to get some wonder of the world leaf, pound it, place it on his chest, and then wrap him up. Then I fell back down and went to sleep.

The wonder of the world leaf is a green leaf shaped like a heart. Mom grew it close to the rose garden and always kept some in the kitchen. Whenever we had a headache, Mom would warm it over the stove, rub some soft candle on, apply it on our forehead, and then tie it down. Shortly thereafter, our head would stop hurting. The kids at school would write their request on it and place it their books. They would have a field day seeing the wonder of the world leaf grew inside their school books.

The next day, Lenny got up and began talking to Mom. We were on Christmas vacation from school, but Christmas was the last thing on our minds. He had already passed the time the doctor said he was going to die, and Mom said it was all in God's hands. We were aware that time was slowly slipping away from Lenny, and we felt helpless. We wanted to spend every second we could with him. He told Mom he wanted a guitar for Christmas. He loved country and Western music. He also loved singing hymns, especially whenever he was drawing a picture of

Jesus or the chalice. Mom wondered if he would remember how to play the guitar. When he was much smaller, the one he had broke. He was a fast learner. Mom got him a guitar and showed him how to play the strings and follow the directions. Soon he was playing beautiful music. With his cowboy hat on, he looked very handsome. We all joined him in singing his favorite songs.

When we were all through singing, he began to sing, "Just as I am without one plea, that thy blood was shed for me." In the middle of the hymn, he stopped and said to Mom, "When I die, I don't want you to worry. I'll be going to heaven." He then said he wanted her to look for him three days after he died. Mom calmly asked him what she should look for. Lenny said, "When you see me, you'll know it's me." She replied, "Okay, son." He then went on to tell her he would let her know when it was time for him to leave this world. With tears streaming down her face, Mom said, "Okay, my son." I remember thinking, *if he's going to return three days after he dies, why die in the first place?* I did not know the powerful meaning behind his words until later on.

Mom continued to place the wonder of the world leaf on him, which gave him tremendous relief from the pain he had been enduring. Whenever we had a high temperature, Mom would go into the garden, pick a few leaves of vervine, boil it, and give it to us unsweetened and without cream to drink. Fifteen minutes later, our temperature would be back to normal. We never knew anything about taking medication.

On Christmas, we all had an enjoyable breakfast. Other relatives came to spend the day with us, bringing gifts along with black cake. The neighbors from across the street also stopped by during the day. We all gathered around to listen to and play the parang music that was on the radio. We also sang hymns on that special day. The hymns that Mom taught us to sing were from the hymn book. We were surprised that those same hymns were also playing on the radio. We felt closer to God, listening to his word and scriptures on the radio.

Lenny went on to see New Year's Day. With all the hugs and kisses we shared, we felt in our hearts it was going to be his last New Year. As time went by, I believed Lenny wasn't going to die. He looked stronger and happier every day. We all found the time to walk through the rose garden together and admire the beautiful roses, bridal bouquet, and lilies that Mom planted.

One night, Rover began howling loudly. We took her inside to try to calm her down, when she suddenly burst into Mom's room without warning, jumped on the bed, and began to lick Lenny. Then she lifted her head toward the ceiling and began to howl again. It sounded very scary. We had to take her back to her kennel, and we were unable to sleep that night. She continued to howl until the following morning, and then she finally stopped.

The neighbors from across the street came by the next day and told Mom they heard Rover howling and that she should prepare herself because it meant there would be a death shortly in the family. Mom became emotional, and they took turns embracing her. When we finally got used to having Lenny around, the day finally arrived—five months after Mom was told by the doctor that Lenny would die within a month's time. Lenny needed to speak to each one of us in private. First he wanted to speak to Carlos, the boy who threw the rock at him. Mom sent Mindy to bring Carlos with his mom. Mindy returned shortly thereafter and told Mom his mother said she was too sick to bring him. At the time, he was suspended from school. Mom sent Mindy back to tell his mother if she didn't want any trouble, to bring her butt and her son over immediately. Mindy returned with both Carlos and his mom. Carlos went in to talk to Lenny as requested. We'll never know what was said. It was a very tense moment with all eyes staring at his mother. God knows what Lenny told Carlos. He bolted out the door, crying as he ran down the path across the river leading to his home. His mother was slowly following him, calling out for him to wait for her. I overheard Lenny tell Mitch, my younger brother, "Everything I have, I share it with you, and you keep losing it. I'm giving you my ring. Please don't lose it." Lenny told Mom how much he loved her and thanked her for having the patience in caring for him. He went on to tell her she was weary and he wanted her to rest now. He said it was time for him to go to heaven. He reminded her not to forget to look out for him, promising he'd return shortly and that he'd be watching over her. Mom began to cry uncontrollably.

It was my turn. He wanted me to promise him I would take care of Mom when he was gone, and he assured me that he'd be watching over me. He told me not to be afraid when I saw the sign. I promised him I would take care of Mom, but I kept thinking that at my age I needed her to take care of me instead. I never realized his request would be granted throughout the coming years. I didn't hear what he said to Mindy, my oldest sister. I didn't want to know; it was all too heavy for my little heart. After talking to Mindy, he told Mom it was time. Mom told Mindy to get the priest. My loving sister ran as fast she could to the rectory. It wasn't too far from where we lived, but it was quite a distance on foot. My heart began to beat very fast. Mom held him in her arms, while Mitch and I gathered around his bed, weeping and singing the hymns, "Rock of Ages," "Blessed Assurance," "Precious Lord, take my hand, lead me, let me stand," "I need thee every hour, I need thee," "Sweet Hour of Prayer," "I Surrender All, I Surrender." Jesus was taking Lenny home to heaven, and there was nothing we could do about it. We felt helpless; my heart was racing faster and faster. Mitch was screaming, stomping, and calling out his brother's name over and over, pleading with him, "Please don't die, please don't die." Meanwhile, Mom held onto her son's body, close to her heart, singing hymn after hymn from deep within her soul, clutching her son to her, never wanting to ever let him go. The time was nearing, and Father Michael wasn't there yet. Mom checked his pulse; he was still alive but barley holding on. I kept praying that Father Michael would make it on time. He was aware of Lenny's fate; he wanted to give him the final rite. Mom poured her heart and soul into every hymn we sang as Lenny lay in her arms with a smile on his face. Mom checked his pulse again; he was holding on to dear life, waiting for Father Michael.

It was a beautiful sunny day with a clear blue sky. The birds were whistling as they flew around the house. They seemed to know what was happening. Meanwhile, we were devastated. Mindy finally arrived with the priest. They had run the whole way and were out of breath. The priest stood facing Lenny as he lay in Ma's arms. With his special scarf around his neck, Father Michael said his prayers with us joining him. He blessed Lenny and muttered the special words under his breath. When he was through giving him the final rite, he walked over to the side of Lenny and placed his arm around him. Lenny gasped and took his final breath. Lenny died peacefully in the arms of both Ma and the priest, with a smile on his face.

Father Michael was not convinced he was dead. He asked Mindy for a mirror and placed it underneath Lenny's mouth. After several minutes of not seeing the fog on the mirror, he was finally convinced that Lenny was indeed dead. The smile on Lenny's face left us speechless—and the fact that he actually had died. We all began screaming out his name, touching, feeling, pulling at him, trying to get him to wake up, but he never did. It seemed to be a bad dream; even though we knew he was going to die, we still didn't expect he would. We didn't rationalize that day would come; yet, it did. It was too late. God had taken him to be on the other side at the tender age of eleven years old. He died on Ma's birthday; yes, indeed, on Ma's birthday, the fourteenth of May. God and his angels took our beloved brother to heaven. He giveth life, and he taketh away, and the time he chose was the right time. He was a special, loving child, whom every mother would be proud to call her son. He didn't live long enough to become a priest on earth, but we're sure he's an angel in heaven, smiling down on us. Mom finally broke down crying, and Father Michael had to help Mom let go of Lenny as she held tightly to his limp body.   The neighbors from across the street had seen the priest coming home with Mindy, so soon they all gathered at our home. Word spread throughout the village and at school. It was not long after his death that the children from the school he attended, including Carlos, flocked around the yard to pay their respects. They were all in shock; Carlos began to cry out, telling everyone he killed

Lenny. Mom had to console him. She told him it was an accident, and she hoped he would learn a valuable lesson from this terrible incident and to remember the tragedy that occurred from the consequences of his reckless action. The other kids wanted to beat up Carlos. Mindy had to go outside and restore peace and order among the children. They kept repeating his name, saying it's not possible he could have died so young. But he did die peacefully with a bright smile on his face. No longer was he going to suffer. No more pain, no more sorrow, maybe a brighter tomorrow.

Mindy sent telegrams to the relatives overseas, including Daddy. The wake was emotional. Relatives came in from near and far, even from London, but Dad never came. Instead, he sent a check to Mom to help with funeral expenses. We later found out that Dad had a fear of travelling, both by sea and air. The neighbors brought coffee, biscuits, and cheese. Even though Mom grew her own coffee, she could not have gone to the field. Mom looked so pale and weak. She had just lost her child, without Dad or any of her in-laws at her side. She was devastated. At the wake, everybody kept talking about what a wonderful boy he was and the good job Mom did raising him along with her other children. The neighbors, who were older and wiser than Mom, advised her not to attend the funeral of her son; it was their traditional belief that whenever a child dies, should the mother attend the funeral, her other children will die one after the other. To abide by their tradition, Mom had to have her minor children crossed over the coffin. A relative lifted us, one by one, and crossed us over Lenny's coffin. It was their strong belief that by doing so, no matter what happens, a mother will not lose another child.

Uncle Randolph, a cardiologist residing in London, received the news by telegram and then passed it on to other relatives. Uncle Randolph came over, along with other relatives. They were there with Mom. Grandpa and other members of the family stood with Mom as well. The announcement of Lenny's death came on over the radio. The doctor who had threatened to call the police on Mom asked her consent to attend the funeral, and his request was granted. There was no time for animosity. It was a time for healing.

The church was packed with many people, including the children from school, along with their parents. The nurses from the ward at the hospital were also there. Even Dr. Marshall wept openly at the service. Some people from the village came out of curiosity to see the child that predicted his own death. The people who could not get inside the church were waiting at the cemetery. Mindy held on to her younger brother and sister's hands, making sure we were safe, protecting us from the huge crowd at the church and the cemetery. At the grave site, I was overcome with grief. It was unbearable to accept the fact that my beloved special brother was gone and never coming back. Other members of the family had to hold me back from attempting to jump into the hole with him. It was heart-wrenching for me.

Soon after Lenny died, Mom was bedridden; her blood pressure had dropped very low. The physician was concerned for her physical well-being. He advised her that if she wasn't careful, she would be next to die. He saw her at home on a regular basis. Uncle Randolph, being a cardiologist, took over and monitored Mom closely. Grandpa was also concerned; he stayed with us to be sure all was okay with Mom and my siblings. Even though we lived in a coco house, it was very big with large rooms. Mom treasured all of Lenny's drawings and paintings, and even his clothes. It was very emotional for Mom to part with his personal things.

Shortly after Lenny's death, Carlos got expelled from school. As time passed, Carlos turned his life around and became a productive member of society. Now and then, he would check in with Ma to see how she was doing. He would surprise her by trimming the branches of the bamboo trees, which were blocking the sunlight from coming into the house. His parents didn't have any legal problems with him anymore.

The day after Lenny's funeral, the family, along with neighbors and friends, came over every night to pray for fourteen nights; they continued to pray for Lenny's soul to rest in peace. This was the traditional way after a loved one died.

Three days after Lenny died, Mindy was preparing lunch, Mitch was playing the guitar, and I was doing the dishes when Mom cried out to us to come and see our brother. We all dropped what we were doing and ran to Mom's room. We were all excited to see Lenny again but didn't know what to expect. When we got to Mom's room, I looked around and didn't see Lenny. Mitch and Mindy just stood there, staring at Mom. I asked Mom, "Where's Lenny?" She pointed to her face as she lay there recuperating; on her face was an unusual looking fly we had never seen before. It was drying up the tears on Mom's face. It was all over her. I took the newspaper and swatted the fly away. I told Mom this stupid-ness could not be my brother. My siblings just stood there staring at the fly. It flew away but then came right back, this time on my face and arms. I started screaming, and Mom reassured me and told me not to be afraid. After a few minutes of enduring the fly all over me, it then flew back to Mom and continued to dry the tears from her eyes. I could not understand any of it. Eventually, I asked Mom, "Is that what Lenny meant when he said he'd be back in three days after he died?" After she said yes, my next question was, "Why a fly?" Mom let me know that when we die, our body dies, but our spirit lives on. If we live a clean and righteous life on earth, God—who created the world and we the people to live in his world, along with the birds, the bees, the flies, the butterflies, the pigeons, crickets, doves, and other creatures, in six days and six nights—will decide which creature one will be recreated into as an angel to help protect their loved ones on earth, especially when they need help the most.

Just as God can see and knows everything before it happens, or what is about to happen in our lives, he chose to send Lenny, not only as a fly, but as an angel looking like a fly, to watch and help protect over his loved ones from heaven. Mom went on to explain to me, "God has every living creature on earth serve a reason and a purpose. God decides who goes to heaven or hell—which is a fiery place no one wants to go to when they die, but will depending on the cruel things they have done to mankind, especially to children. There's certainly a place in hell awaiting them. God is a supernatural being we cannot see; however, he can see each and every one of us on earth. He knows what's in our hearts and in our minds and what we are planning to do, even before we do it. He decides who or what creature should be our guardian angel." I asked Mom why Lenny said to look for him three days after he died. Why not four or five days after? She said to me, "When we die, our spirit is raised on the third day, as Jesus did. Before Jesus was viciously crucified on the cross, he walked the face of the earth as a human being performing many miracles. He even walked on water without getting his feet wet. Three days after he died, he rose from the dead, not as a human being, but as a supernatural being we cannot see or touch, but who can see and touch us. He can even raise us from our dying bed, depending on if we believe in him. He chooses who should live or die, to do his work in heaven or on earth."

I missed my beloved brother terribly. I needed to see and talk to my brother as a human being, not as a fly. I explained that to my mom. Mom told me to ask God for what I wanted in life. If he sees what's best for me, he'll let me have it. She went on to let me know that God tends to answer little children's prayers faster than adults'. I asked her why, and she replied, "Because God said, 'Suffer not, thy little children, to come unto me.' Children are very precious and are innocent human beings; they are special gifts and blessings from God."

Mom became concerned and started paying closer attention to me. Mindy and Mitch were grieving in their silent way, while I was praying, asking God to please send my brother back to earth for me to talk to. I went on to let him know how much I was grieving for him.

It was time to return to school. Life seemed to stand still for Mitch and me.

One bright sunny Monday morning, instead of playing with the other kids, I went into the church, which was opposite the school, and prayed for a miracle. Each day, my tender heart grieved for my brother. I would visit his grave, which was above the schoolyard. Mom had placed a tombstone on his grave. It was easy for me to recognize it with the special engraving. I would bring flowers from the rose garden and place them on his grave while I cleaned the weeds. I would talk to him, reminding him how much I loved and missed him. Even though I told him how much I was hurting, I'm sure he knew how much I was suffering deep inside. Losing him was losing a best friend, a rare diamond.

One day; as I stood at the side of the door of the church, admiring how handsome the boys looked in their new uniforms—white shirts, black pants, and a black tie instead of blue shirts and khaki pants—I could not believe my eyes. There was a young boy who was the spitting image Lenny, walking into the schoolyard. I ran home as fast as I could to tell Ma what I had just seen. She asked me if I was sure he resembled Lenny. I assured her, and Mom and I ran all the way back to the school. When we got there, the bell had already rung and the kids were back in their classes from recess.

Mom instructed me to meet her at the side door of the church when classes were let out for lunch at noon. I could hardly compose myself. At lunch break, I joined Ma at the side door of the church, waiting for the boy to emerge from school. Mitch joined us as we waited patiently. Finally, the young boy came out from the schoolyard, approached us, and said, "Good day." He was about to enter the church. Mom could not believe her eyes.

The young man was indeed the spitting image of Lenny. She was speechless, except to say, "Oh my God." Mom then broke down crying. The young boy, Ray, was unaware of what was happening. He politely asked Ma what was wrong. Ray thought he had said something inappropriate to her. Mom composed herself and told him of his strong resemblance to her son, who had recently died. Roslyn, his sister, joined the conversation. Ray explained to us that they had recently moved into the district with their parents. They were living much further up from where we lived. They both walked with their lunches in "carriers." They said they were getting teased by the other children about what was provided for them and that they had to eat in the church. Mom invited the children to have lunch with us. It was a miracle. My prayers had been answered. We could not stop staring at Ray, who was a Godsend to help heal our emotional pain. Ray was the same age as Lenny.

Ma wanted to meet Ray's parents. She sent a note requesting to meet with them, and the parents obliged. She explained Lenny's death and Ray's strong resemblance to him. It was the beginning of a remarkable and beautiful friendship. Throughout the years, the families kept in touch with each other. We sometimes would all have dinner together. Each day after school, Ray and his sister would come over to visit Mom, and she always gave them fruits and vegetables to take to their family. They were not as fortunate as we were. As time went on, Ray found himself a beautiful young lady and fell in love. He brought her home to get Mom's approval. I remember when he called Ma into the kitchen to ask her what she thought of her. Mom laughed, and it was the first time I heard her laugh since Lenny's death. She always looks so sad. Mom gave him her blessing and wished them God's continued blessings, along with a few words of wisdom. She felt honored that he cared enough to introduce her to his girlfriend.

Ray got married and moved to Canada. Later on, he sent Mom pictures of his three beautiful children. His sister, Roslyn, eventually fell in love, got married, and continued to live not far from her parents and Mom. With God's help, my family and I found the emotional strength and will power to carry on with our lives. We were blessed to have had the opportunity to meet Ray and his family. Joy and happiness came back into our lives, and God knew that in our hearts, we were emotionally healed.

chapter 3

Shortly after Lenny's death, Mom went to Grenada in another attempt to see Cindy, her second child. She finally saw her. Mom said it was the first time Cindy learned she had a biological mother and siblings. Mom was allowed to see her for only a short amount of time, but the happiness she felt meeting her long lost child for the first time in several years gave Mom the determination to fight to get her daughter back.

When Mom came home, she spent most of her time working in the garden. Mindy was working and attending school, majoring in shorthand and typing. She helped Mom financially whenever she could. Mom would head to the garden at 6:00 a.m. and return at 8:00 a.m. to prepare breakfast for Mitch and me before she took us to school. She would then go home, make lunch, and head back to the garden. She would take us back to school after lunch and then would head back to the garden until we returned from school at 3:00 p.m. I sometimes watched Mom with her long pants tucked into her tall galoshes, armed with a cutlass, rake , shovel, and hoe, placed in a wheelbarrow, as she crossed over the ravine and walked up the hill to cut down the thick branches of trees that stood in the way of her planting the vegetables. With each stroke, she called on Jesus to give her the strength, courage, and endurance to make it through the blistering heat. She even had to cut down the tall bamboo trees that prevented sunlight from coming into the house. Mom would tie a thick rope around the trunk of the tree and then cut the branches off one by one. Then she would cut the trunk of the tree until she was sure it was ready to come down. She would then pull and tug with all her might in the direction she wanted the tree to fall. Finally, she would clean up all the branches she had cut down. Mitch and I would cheer her on and praise her for being so strong and brave. I felt sorry for her and prayed that someday things would get better. There were times; I felt Mom was wasting her time cutting down, those tall thick trees to plant vegetables.

Our chores were to water the garden on a daily basis. With time, patience, and the right care, before we knew it, we had a large vegetable garden. We were very proud of Mom. We had corn, red and green peppers, pigeon peas, tomatoes, green fig, dasheen, dasheen bush, pumpkin, mangoes, sapodillas, sugar cane, sugar apple, passion fruits, avocadoes, pomarack, guavas, oranges, sapodilla, bananas, white and yellow yams, sweet potatoes, lemons, limes, sour oranges, coco, coffee, sage, mint, eddoes, and cucumbers. Mom showed us how to grow watercress and lettuce at the side of the ravine. The coffee was so plentiful that Mom would fill a bag and give it to the neighbors across the river. She never sold any of it. Mom didn't have to buy cotton. She grew her own. We took pleasure in picking the cotton. The more fruits and vegetables Mom gave away, the more God blessed her with.

Mom was always praying, including first thing in the morning and last thing at night. She told me and Mitch to always address Mindy as Sister Mindy as a sign of love and respect for her. To this day, we sometimes still address her as sister. On many occasions, we would leave for school on a beautiful sunny day, only to return home for lunch to find the river overflowing its banks. Mitch and I would be dumbfounded, asking each other how we were going to get home. At the other end of the riverbank, Mom would call out, "Don't move a muscle!" She would be waiting, which made us feel safe. Mom would be standing with her tall galoshes on, her head scarf, and her waist banded. In her hand, she held a long rod, pushing it hard into the water, measuring the depth as she warbled herself from side to side, battling the thick brown water to get across to her children. Mom would take Mitch first, since he was the youngest, advising him to hold on tightly around her neck. Mitch found it to be funny to be on Mom's back and would say, "Come on, horsy." Mom would take it all in stride, advising him to keep still before they both fell in the water. Next it was my turn. Once we were safe at home, we had to wash our hands before eating. Mom always emphasized the importance of hygiene and proper etiquette. After lunch, depending on the depth of the water, Mom would take us on her back all over again across the river and back to school. Should the river get heavier while we were at school, she would take a longer route to get us home. She needed her children to study and focus on their education. There was no excuse for not attending school, except illness. When she returned from school with us in the afternoon, sometimes the mucky water would have gone down a bit, but there wouldn't be any stones for us to walk over on. We would find Mom lifting heavy stones above her head to put back in place so we could cross over the river.

Even though there was no electricity at home, at nights the house was always bright. Mitch and I took turns cleaning the lamp shades, wetting newspaper to clean the inside the shade. Mom always made sure there was enough oil in the lamp for us to do our homework and study. She also made sure we had a snack of biscuits, homemade guava jelly, and a glass of cow's milk before we studied. Uncle David was also an agriculturist. Besides working at the ministry of agriculture, he also had his own farm, rearing animals, including cows and goats. He always brought cow and goat milk for us. We were only allowed to play in the big yard in front of the house when we were through studying, under the watchful eye of Mom. Every evening at 6:00, Mom would call us in from playing to give us a bath before dinner. When she was through washing our hair and bathing us, she would massage us from head to toe with olive oil or coconut oil, which she made. After dinner, Mom would pray with us. We had to take turns praising and thanking God for his many wonderful blessings. We also had to pray for the people around the world, including those who were in various homes, hospitals, and institutions.

One night while praying, I interrupted the prayers and asked why we had to pray for people around the world we don't know. Mom explained that people around the world needed prayers for peace, daily bread, good health, and whatever problems they were facing. She went on to tell me that the Lord says where the twos and the threes are gathered together in prayer, he's definitely in the midst. I understood quite clearly and didn't complain any more. Mom continued to instill in us the importance of saying please and thank you. She said to always knock on a door before entering, advising us to never open a door unless we heard the words "come in." She said to never sit down unless we were told to sit. She went on to let us know, "Fashions may come and go, but manners never go out of style." She emphatically said that good manners and education go hand in hand.

chapter 4

My pediatrician referred my mom to an ear nose and throat specialist for me. Before I continue, I wish to emphasize that regardless of how tired, angry, frustrated, or emotionally drained you may feel with your child, please never raise, tug, pull, or drag your child by one hand up in the air. Always place both your hands under both of the child's armpits. Lifting a child up by one hand can cause a serious ear infection. If the infection goes undetected, it can cause the child to be hard of hearing or become deaf.

Mom would have to wake me up at 3:00 a.m. to go see the specialist in San Fernando. Before leaving, Mindy made sandwiches and homemade cocoa for us to take with us. The night before, Mindy would comb my hair and tie it down to make sure it looked good the following day. There were so many times Mom and I arrived at the hospital before the appointed time to see the specialist, only to be told he wasn't in or wouldn't be coming in that day. His nurse would look at Mom from head to toe and then tell her Dr. Mohammed wouldn't be coming in. She would give Mom another date and time to return. Mom continued to get rejected over and over again. Dr. Mohammed was not only the top ear, nose, and throat specialist, he was also rich and famous. No one could see him unless the patient was rich or had a referral from a reputable pediatrician.

One particular morning, it was raining heavily. I didn't want to get up, but I had to try to see the specialist one more time. Sister Mindy got up to make sure all was okay with us before heading out the door. She made sure Mom and I had on our rain hats and rain coats. Before leaving, Mom would ask God to take us to and from our destination safely and to open a way for me to see the doctor. She often took her large flashlight to flash around the front yard. Leaving home that early in the morning, the flashlight was our guiding light to safety, to be sure there were no strangers or frogs hoping around. Mom would hold my hand as we headed toward the path leading across the river. Rover, the dog, would go in front of us to make sure all was well. In the stillness of the morning, we could hear the frogs making their funny noises as we headed to the street to wait for public transportation to take us on our long journey.

We arrived at the hospital and were turned away once again, with another appointed date and time. This time, Mom broke down and cried. I remember leaving the hospital and seeing many fancy cars heading in the direction of Dr. Mohammed's private office. I thought maybe we were too poor to see him. When we got on the bus to go home, I rested my head in Mom's arms and felt very safe. I silently made a promise to her that someday I'd make her proud of me and she would not have to cry anymore. I was determined to succeed in life. I was not going to let poverty or being hard of hearing keep me down. When we got home, I told Mom I no longer wanted to see the specialist. It was just too humiliating to be turned away over and over again.

Mom continued to take Mitch and me to the pediatrician for our routine examination. On one occasion, Dr. Earthen learned that I had not seen the specialist. She immediately got on the phone and spoke to Dr. Mohammed about the many times Mom and I had been turned away. He claimed he was unaware of the situation. She insisted that he see me as soon as possible, and he gave her a date and time for me to return to his office. I told my pediatrician I didn't want Mom and me to be humiliated anymore. She said she didn't want me to be scared and let me know it was crucial for me to see the doctor. She didn't want the infection from my ear going up to my brain and affecting my studying.

At school, I tried my best to do well. Meanwhile, I was hiding a dark secret from Mom. At twelve years old, I was afraid to attend school because of the beatings I endured from the bullies in my class. Being a shy kid, I had to endure being called skinny, deaf, and stupid. During recess, I wanted to stay in the classroom and read. The teacher, who was very strict, made it clear to me she didn't want anyone in the classroom during recess. She never asked me what was wrong or why I wanted to stay in during recess. She wanted all students to go outside and play. While the other kids played, I would go into the church and pray, asking God, along with the other saints in heaven, to protect me from the bullies and to help me make it through the day. The leader of the pack was short, but she was also tough and aggressive. The other kids followed her around like puppets on a string. My friends Tasha and Wendy always stood up for me. Whenever they were around, they made sure the leader of the pack and her gang didn't get close to me. Tasha began to fall behind in her studies. She confided in me that her mom had cancer and she had to help care for her. Sometimes after school on Fridays, Tasha would come to my home, and asked my mom's permission for me to spend time with her. Mom consented but with strict instructions that I return home before 6:00 p.m.

During my visit to Tasha's home, I realized how tough it was for her to focus on her homework. She didn't have much time. Whenever she didn't attend school, I missed her terribly. We grew up together and didn't live too far from each other. She also lived across a river. She was one of the few friends I trusted to watch my back. The bullies respected her more than they did Wendy. Surrounding me, they would have the nerve to ask me where my bodyguard was. When you are surrounded by five tough kids bigger than you are, besides being scared, you learn to be even more humble and take whatever physical abuse they dish out.

There were so many times I had to run into the church and hide from the bullies. I could actually hear my heart beating as I hid between the church pews. They would find me and pounce on my head, right there and then in the church. On one particular day during recess, I ran as fast as I could down the school stairs and into the church to hide. With the bullies following closely behind me, I hid behind the statue of St. Anthony. I could hear my heart racing faster and faster. My knees were buckling underneath me, trembling from fear. I cried out to him to protect me from the gang. I made him a promise that if he did, when I grew older, I would enter the convent and serve God for the rest of my life. As I hid behind the statue, I could see them as they entered the church, looking around between the pews, asking each other, "Where did she go?" I silently prayed that they wouldn't find me. My frail body was tired from the beatings. During their search, the bell rang and they left. I thanked St. Anthony for protecting me and then looked through the window from the church and saw my classmates standing in line to go upstairs. The bullies were looking around in every direction for me. I waited until the kids began walking up the stairs; then I came out and fell in behind them. When they got into the classroom, they kept asking each other, "Where was she hiding?"

I couldn't tell Mom what was happening because the leader of the pack, Brandy, had threatened to do bodily harm to my family and me, should I tell my mom or anyone else. She even told me she knew my father didn't live at home, and it would be easier for her and her friends to come and go without anyone finding out. I allowed fear to overpower me; I had forgotten Rover was there, and she would have certainly taken care of them.

I dreaded having to go to school. Sometimes I wished I could just crawl under the covers and never get up, but that was only wishful thinking. I had to get my education. Mom was always making special food for us. After school, she always insisted we take off our uniform before having a snack. She made sure we washed our hands before and after every meal and brushed our teeth. Mom made delicious guava jelly, which we would spread on our sandwiches. We were only allowed to have a limited amount of guava cheese. She was concerned we would get worms from eating too many sweets. Mom always made sure she gave us a dose of castor oil to cleanse our system. We disliked the taste of it, but she said it was good for our health.

One day when I returned from school, Mom was stuffing the fibers into the cover of a queen-size mattress. As soon as she was through putting all the fibers into the mattress, she then sewed it back up with her long needle. I kissed her, dropped my bag, and headed out the door without getting her permission to go outside and play. I felt terrible, having had another day with the kids pulling my ponytails, punching, and cuffing me on the back of my head. As soon as our teacher stepped out of the room, they would let me have it. It had given me such a terrible headache, I needed to get away. I needed to play and talk to someone. I needed to feel free as a bird. I went over to Tasha's home; she didn't attend school that day. We played hopscotch for a while and talked about the events that took place at school. Mom got concerned when she didn't see me in the living room. When I got back home at 6:00 p.m., Mom was standing at the front door. Before I could kiss her, she took me into the living room and said, "Young lady, where have you been, and where did you come from?" When I was through telling her, she gave me a strict warning to never let it happen again. She needed to know our every move. She sent me to kneel down in the corner of my room, with my hands in the air, and ask God to forgive me for what I did wrong, causing her to worry.

Mom was a loving mother who made her children her top priority. She gave us love, security, and stability. She wanted us to walk the straight and narrow path in life, and she didn't want us to get in trouble with the law. She would say, "I'm not going to spare the rod and spoil the child." She taught us to have self-discipline. She taught us that we couldn't always have what we wanted, whenever we wanted it. Mom attended services mostly on Thursdays and Sundays. Sometimes during the holidays, she would take us with her. She loved to surprise us by taking us with her, which we enjoyed very much. Before doing so, we had to go bed early because the drive would be long. Mom wanted to be sure we were rested.

During the trip, members of the church would sing and clap, even playing the Hawaiian organ, which was just beautiful, praising the Lord on our journey until we arrived at our destination. On Sunday mornings, when Mitch and I returned from service, Mindy would be preparing breakfast. From across the river, we could smell it. Mom made sure we all had our meals together. Her motto was, "The family that prays together, stays together." Mom reared chickens, fowls, and turkeys. On weekends, Mitch and I fed them with chick feed, along with turkey feed, and then we had to clean up their coop. During the week, Mom would be up to feed them first, before heading off to the garden. Grandpa even bought pigeons for Ma as pets to care for. We were kept busy with our chores. On Sundays for lunch, Mom and Mindy would prepare a fowl she reared and macaroni pie. The chicken tasted so good. Mom and Mindy certainly knew how to cook. Mom usually picked a bunch of ripe bananas and placed them in a tray on the table along with mangoes or oranges. The bananas would remain for several days before we ate them. Just the sweet aroma coming from the fruits made us eat more and more. I often wondered how on earth Ma did it as a single parent with two teenagers and an adult child.

One Sunday when Mitch and I returned from Sunday mass, which started at 6:00 a.m., Mindy was preparing breakfast. She called me into the kitchen and told me not to go up to the altar to receive Holy Communion the next time I attended service. I asked her why not, and she replied, "Because the members of the congregation will see the big hole under the sole of your shoe." She told me to wait until Mom or Dad bought me a new pair before going back to receive Communion. I felt a bit embarrassed and told her the Lord said, "Render your heart and not your garment." I always admired Mindy for being alert and caring about us. Whenever she was down from her job and her studies in Siparia, she always made sure everything was all right with us. Whenever there was a hole in our shoe and Mom could not afford to buy a pair right away, she would measure the size of the shoe and place a piece of cardboard inside it. Dad would ask Mom to take measurements of our feet and send it to him. Mom would get a piece of cardboard and have each of us place our feet on it, and with a pen she would draw the size of each foot, cut it, write our names on it, and send it to him. Dad was a penny pincher. He watched how he spent every nickel and dime. Instead of sending the money for Mom to buy the shoes, he would buy them himself. He believed by doing so, they would last longer. Sometimes he would buy the exact size, and on other occasions he would send them a little too big. Mom would have to stuff tissues inside to get a good fit. The shoes he sent us were brand-new leather shoes. He would let us know he bought a larger size because they would last longer. Instead of being grumpy, we were appreciative that he took the time to send them. Classmates would comment on how they knew the shoes were not from this country because of the scent of the leather. We felt proud that though Dad was not there in person, he still paid attention to us.

It was very important for Mom to teach us the difference between a good touch and a bad touch by demonstrating the right and wrong way. Should anyone touch us in an inappropriate way, we were to let her know. When I was fourteen, sex education was taught to my class. I could not wait to tell Mindy what I had learned. Shortly after I arrived home, I told her what I learned about sex. I suddenly heard a stern voice from behind me say, "Match and take a book." It was the beginning and the end of the subject. It was never discussed it in the presence of Mom again. God bless the day Mom told me to match and take a book. From that day on, I read on a regular basic. I soon realized the importance of reading. Ma didn't have her mother or anyone else to discuss the subject with her, and because of the emotional, psychological, and mental abuse she experienced from men, she didn't feel comfortable discussing the subject. Mom was a private person. We never saw her thighs until she was very ill. Mom was always respectful of her body, and she wanted us to respect our bodies. Even though we may have been financially poor, we felt richly blessed on a daily basis.

Mom always told us, "Poverty is not a crime, it's a challenge, and we can rise above it." She wanted us to focus on our education and to succeed academically. She made sure we read the newspaper regularly or a good book. Regardless, of how tired or physically hurting Mom was from working in the garden, she always found the time to ensure our needs were met. She had very little time for herself. Mom didn't socialize much. On one occasion, we all attended a birthday party for one of her friends from church. She was asked to dance, and while dancing, she suddenly paused and asked the gentleman to wait a minute; her leg had begun to cramp. We all had a good laugh at the time but later realized how much pain Mom was in.

chapter 5

Mitch was a very intelligent kid. He was doing well at school and was preparing for the common entrance examination. The board of education decided it was in the best interest of the children who were preparing for the examination to have more time to study by remaining after school. The principal had confidence in Mitch. He needed Ma's permission to have him stay after school to get extra help. She agreed. Mom made sure she was right there to meet him after class. I had already taken the examination and failed. There were no after-school programs at the time. Only one student from our class passed. I felt disappointed, but I knew there were other ways I could succeed in life.

One bright and beautiful Monday morning, Mom took us to school before heading off to the garden. When we arrived, Mom kissed Mitch and me good-bye and waited for me to get to the top of the stairs. As soon as I got to the top of the stairs, fear overpowered me. I could not go into my classroom. I waited until Mom was out of sight, and then I ran down the stairs as fast as I could and headed home. When I got there, Mom was already in the garden. I just crawled into bed with my uniform and shoes on and hid under the covers. Whenever I was called upon by the teacher to answer a question, I was told to shut up. I was unable to express myself verbally anymore. Praying with the rest of the family gave me the courage to express myself without fear, which made it easier for me to express my experiences at school.

I was awakened by the tapping of feet; Mom needed to know why I was at home and not at school. I told her I had a headache. She said that was not a good enough answer. She needed to know the truth, the whole truth, and nothing but the truth. I broke down and told Mom what had been happening at school with the bullies. She was very upset with me for not telling her sooner. She got me a glass of water to drink, and then she removed her galoshes, dressed in a conservative manner, took my hand, and headed for the door. I asked her where we were going, and she said, "Back to school." Scared as a rabbit, I told Ma the kids would beat me up again. My mom replied, "Oh no! After today, they are not going to anymore."

We arrived late. All the students' eyes were on Mom and me as we headed for the principal's office. I felt a bit embarrassed. Mom was always a cool, calm, and collected person. She once said to me that as a parent, you have to learn to control yourself at all times. Hastiness will not get you anywhere. You have to set a good example for your child so that when they grow older and have children of their own, they will know how to conduct themselves in any situation. I can still remember her exact words to the principal. She said, "I'm sending my child to school to get an education, not to be beaten up on." The principal wanted to know who the kids were and how long it had been going on. I broke down and told her who the kids were, when it started, and all about the threats, the name calling, and the beatings, especially to the back of my head. I had been having a lot of headaches. For two years, the bullies had taken my freedom from me. They violated me. It only took my mom a few minutes to help me gain back my freedom and feel safe for the first time in a while. A heavy burden lifted from my heart. My mom finally knew the truth. The principal called in my teacher and asked if she was aware of what had been going on with me in regards to the bullies. She said she wasn't, and I had to tell her what I had been enduring. I felt brave enough to remind her that when I tried to stay in the classroom during recess, instead of asking me if anything was wrong, she sent me outside into the hands of the bullies. The bullies were called in and questioned. They began to accuse each other. Their parents were also called in.

I was unaware that prior to this, my pediatrician had given Mom a letter to take to the principal. After my physical examination, she excused Mom from the room and questioned me. She wanted to know how I was doing at school and if I was having any problems with the kids at school. But my answer to her was always that I was doing fine. Mom was called back into the room, and the doctor spoke to her in private. Pediatricians are qualified to know if a child is being abused in any way. The child's facial expression, eye contact, and body language can tell a story before the child is even asked a question. Mom reminded the principal of the letter she had given to her from my pediatrician. She read it again and became serious, and Mom became even more serious. The bullies were expelled from school, and the principal gave the teacher a stern warning. Mom thanked her for her cooperation and said should she hear of anything happening to her child again, she would take it further.

For the first time in a long time, I felt safe at school. I was very proud of Mom for the way she stood up to the principal and the parents of the bullies, asking the parents what they were instilling in their children. I admired her for being so brave and carrying herself in a respectable manner. She was a person who stood up for what she believed was right.

No child should ever have to live in fear. We are all God's children; he created us all in his own image and likeness. Bullies have no right to torture other kids. It's time something serious is done about it. A law should be passed holding parents responsible for their children's actions. A parent has to be responsible enough to see some kind of change in their children's behavior. A parent should not be afraid of their own children. If you are afraid of your child, then talk to your parish priest, your pastor, a professional, someone you can trust; don't feel ashamed or afraid if your child is intimidating you. Do the right thing. You may be helping to save your own life and the life of another child. Sooner or later, those who turn a deaf ear instead of protecting the children that God has entrusted into their care will certainly be punished.

Mom taught us that violence is never the answer and that there's a solution to every problem. Instead of fighting, walk away. I looked forward to attending classes every day without fear of being beaten anymore. The other students showed me respect and wanted me to be their friend, but I kept to myself. Mom continued to be right there to meet us after school, even though she had to wait a while longer for Mitch to finish his after-school program. Mom and I would pray for a while at the church. We would then visit Lenny's grave and talk to him in our silent way, asking God to continue to let his soul rest in peace. We would clean the thick weeds off his grave, place beautiful flowers that Mom took from the garden, and then head back down to the school to wait for Mitch. Mom raised us to be strong, to handle whatever life may throw at us. She taught us to keep God close in our lives and to trust and believe in him because he will see us safely through. On our way home from school, we would stop at the post office to check for mail. Mom always looked disappointed when she didn't receive a registered letter from Daddy. At night, when Mom thought we were asleep, I could hear her crying. There were so many nights that the bed shook from her sobs. One night, I thought my head would burst from hearing Mom sobbing and wishing I could take away her pain. I got up and knocked on her door; she immediately stopped crying and quickly opened the door. I told her I had a terrible headache. Mom applied the soft candle on my forehead, placed the wonder of the world leaf on it, and then rocked me in her arms until I fell asleep. I could not wait to grow up to help Mom. Dad would write often and then stop. It was heartbreaking whenever he did that, which was often. Mom taught us to ask God for whatever our hearts desire. "If he sees it's his will, thy will be done. If not, ask him to help us accept the things we cannot change." Whenever Dad sent the allowance to Mom, she made every dollar count. She made sure she bought clothes and vitamins for us. She picked oranges from the tree, squeezed them, and then sweetened the juice with glucose instead of sugar. She even bought Horlicks, Ovaltine, and Milo Tonic. We would have a choice; instead of having homemade cocoa, we would have had Ovaltine or Milo Tonic. But most important was olive oil. Mom would give us a tablespoon of olive oil to drink on a regular basic, which she explained to us was not only to help fight and prevent infections, but also to strengthen our intestines.

Mom even treated us to a movie, *Ben-Hur* or the *Ten Commandments*. It made Mitch and me feel good to know that Mom took time off from the garden to spend an outing with us. Ma was a quiet person, not loud or aggressive. However, she was a straightforward, no nonsense person. She told us we have to show respect to get respect. She would say there's a time and place for everything. She also reminded us that our body is a temple in the spirit of God. Mom was always doing good deeds for the neighbors. One night, on her way home from service, a stray dog followed her all the way home; she was pregnant and hungry. The following morning, when we awoke, Mom told us about the dog. When we saw her, we fell in love with her immediately. We named her Rover. Mom made a doghouse for her. Mom was also good with a hammer and nails. She showed us how to use them. Rover went on to have healthy beautiful puppies, which Mom shared with the neighbors. Mom was there when Rover went into labor and then nursed Rover back to health. Rover became very protective of Mom and the rest of the family. Rover would not go to sleep until Mom arrived home safely after attending service at night. She would lie in front of the door, and as soon as she smelled Mom, she would take off running down the gap and then bring Mom safely home.

During the Christmas season, we wanted to help Ma put up the wallpaper. We needed her to show us how she went about putting it up to make the house looked pretty. Mom had the patience to teach Mitch and me how to paste the glue on the paper, hold it carefully at the tip, place it on the wall, and then gently smooth it out. When we were finished, the entire house looked beautiful. Mom and Mindy did a lot of baking during this time. Mom made bread, sweet bread, and black cake in the oven, which she built outside. It took a lot of time, patience, and endurance, but it was worth it. Mom also baked ham. When she was through cutting off the fat from the ham, she would dress it with cloves. Mitch and I didn't miss having a Christmas tree because we couldn't miss what we didn't have. Mom taught us to be content with what we had and to thank God for the many blessings he bestowed upon us. On Christmas Eve, Mindy and Mom would put up the new curtains. Our home looked beautiful with the long-stem red and white roses on the table, which Mom grew in the rose garden.

Mitch and I always looked forward to Christmas. On Christmas day, when we returned from service, Mom and Mindy prepared breakfast. After an enjoyable breakfast, we were ready for the gifts that Santa Claus left us, which Mom neatly wrapped and placed underneath our beds while we were asleep. Mom would tell us that because we were good throughout the year, Santa Claus brought the gifts we wanted. When we got older, we learned that Mom saved from her allowance to buy our Christmas gifts. Prior to Christmas, Mom would take us to see Mr. and Mrs. Claus in a helicopter that flew over the park. We would have to leave early because many people came from far and wide with their children to see Santa Claus. They would scramble onto the field to get their presents, which were thrown from the helicopter. As time went on, the authorities realized how dangerous it was because of the number of kids that were getting hurt or separated from their parents, so it stopped. Instead, parents took their children to the shopping mall to see Santa Claus, which was much safer. The only time we saw alcohol in our home was during the Christmas holidays or if our relatives were coming to visit from abroad. Mom would place the alcohol in a special cupboard under lock and key.

Whenever the evangelists came to Trinidad to have a crusade revival, regardless of how tired Mom was, she found the time to take us to the service revival, which sometime lasted a few weeks, depending on how many people attended. Their message of hope and trust in God, and their reminder of the many miracles he can perform in our lives on a daily basis, gave the members of the congregation faith to believe in the greatest man that has ever walked the face of the earth. Mom certainly believed that all things are possible for those who believe in God and that it was only a matter of time before I got healed and our financial position got better. Mom continued to motivate us to put our trust and belief in the Lord and to remember that every disappointment that happens in our lives is for a good reason. Mom reminded us that there's a higher power above who watches over each and every one of us; all we need to do is reach out to him and hold onto his unchanging love. Just hold on, keep the faith, and never give up on God. If we continued to do whatever good we could to help those who were less unfortunate than we were, he would continue to shower us with many more blessings. Mom taught us not to do anything for fame because God does not like hypocrites. She let us know that we can fool some of the people some of the time, but we cannot fool all of the people all of the time, especially the righteous ones.

On family day, Mom took the time to lecture us about life, reminding us there are no shortcuts in life. With hard work, self-discipline, patience, determination, perseverance, and endurance, we can accomplish anything we want to. There will be stumbling blocks along the way, but we should never quit or give up on our dreams. She went on to let us know should we fall down, we need to get up, dust ourselves off, and continue on our way. She insisted we should never feel sorry for ourselves. It is okay to cry out to God for his continuous help, but never forget to thank him on a daily basis for the many blessings he has bestowed upon us, including the roof over our heads, the meals on the table, a comfortable bed to sleep on, and our senses. She reminded her children that whenever they think they have it bad, there is someone out there who is even worse off. We learned to be humble and appreciative of the important things in life.

chapter 6

Mom and the principal of the school Mitch attended were disappointed when they learned that Mitch had failed the common entrance examination. The principal realized that Mitch had potential and advised Mom to get him into a private school immediately. They could not afford to give up on him. Mom immediately sent a letter to Dad explaining what was happening. He responded quickly and agreed to pay for Mitch to attend a private high school. Back then, if you didn't pass the common entrance examination to get into high school and your parents couldn't afford a private one, you could go to a vocational school. Dad paid for Mitch to attend the private school for three months.

The following day after Mom received the news that Mitch had failed the exam, she woke up and told us that Mitch did pass the exam. She told us that in her dream, she saw there was a mix up. An error was made, and the truth would come out. During the second month while Mitch was attending Osmond High School, the principal came running down the gap, across the river, into the long and winding road leading to our home. He was out of breath, so Mom offered him a glass water to drink. He was excited to tell her the good news. He brought a letter he had received from the board of education, apologizing to the principal for the error they made in regards to Mitch failing the common entrance examination. He had indeed passed for a prestigious high school. We were all flabbergasted. The principal told Mom to try to get him into the school as soon as possible and to take the letter with her. Everything had to be done in a hurry. Two months had already gone by, and Mom had to get him new uniforms and school supplies. The new school was not using the same uniform or books as the previous school. Mom had to ensure Mitch had money for lunch every day. She didn't receive a refund from the high school that Mitch previously attended. Dad, upon hearing the good news, came through for Mom. He made sure Mitch got the necessary items he needed to attend school. Instead of waiting on Dad's delayed financial help, Mom prepared Sunday meals for the members of her church and did the laundry for her bachelor cousin to bring in extra income, which helped tremendously.   Being the only boy, Mitch realized he had to grow up fast to help Mom out instead of seeing her struggle financially. Mitch would sit at the river for long periods of time. Mom became concerned and asked him why he was spending all his time at the river. He said that he told the river his problems so that the water would wash them all away. Mom said him it was a good thing to do but reminded him that he could also talk to God. Even though God knew what was happening in Mitch's life, he wanted Mitch to reach out to him.

As the holiday approaches, it will be another year since God took Mom away from us. We miss her tremendously; the emotional pain of losing her is incomprehensible. We know she's in heaven with Lenny and Dad, surrounded by angels, looking down upon us, but it will never be the same, getting up in the morning to call her and knowing she's not going to be at the other end of the line. We'll always remember the extraordinary person she was. As a single parent, she raised us to the best of her ability. Mom was concerned for our safety. Whenever the neighbors asked her why she didn't find a man to help her in the garden, she said she had to protect her children. She didn't want anybody moving in with her to molest her children because she would definitely cut off their private parts. I had a good laugh when I heard her say that to the neighbors. I felt very proud of Mom. Her words and actions made me feel even more safe and secure, and this inspired me to be protective of her. She would conclude by saying God would continue to provide; she would do her best, and he would certainly do the rest.

Grandpa showed Mom how to build a chicken coop and raise chickens and turkeys. Mom taught us how to call the chickens by saying, "Chick, chick, it's feeding time." Mitch and I would have a hearty laugh seeing the chicken running toward us for their meal. Mitch and I would take turns cleaning the chicken coop; after scooping up their waste, we would place it at the trunk of the fruits and vegetables, which was used for manure. Every evening, the chicken and turkeys would go to their coops to sleep. If any of the chickens were ill, Mom would take her time and feed the chicken with lemon juice and olive oil. The chickens would lay their brown eggs in the coop or would find a nesting place in the garden. Mom would follow them into their hiding nest, only to be amazed to find dozens of eggs hidden under the branches. Mom would even find small chickens that were already breaking out from their shells. She could not let the turkeys or the fowls know she found their nest; otherwise, they would move on to another hiding place. Mom always knew the difference between the fowls and the turkeys' eggs because the turkey eggs were long.

Mom sometimes would catch crayfish, crabs, or lobster, under the stones in the water, which would be a thrill for us. She even showed us how they were cooked, and then she would serve them to us. One day while cleaning the garden, Mom discovered a hole containing clay. She showed us how to make a vase and other ornaments from clay, which we found to be messy yet fascinating. One of the neighbors from across the street was a struggling artist. He asked Mom if he could have some of the clay, and she said of course. She never charged him. However, he got greedy and kept carrying out the clay in large containers to his home. He finally emptied the hole. When he completed his work of art, he invited us to the opening of his art gallery near his home, with beautiful ornaments he made from the clay. They were magnificent. Tourists stopped by to admired his beautiful work. He did very well from the sale of his products. He even got orders to make more of. And again, he kept returning for more clay. Each time the whole refilled, there he was again. We insisted that Mom stop him because enough was enough; we needed to make our own products, but she sympathized with him because he had a family to feed. We understood. We were humbly grateful for the many blessings that God had bestowed upon us, which others didn't have.

On mornings, it was breathtaking to walk outside and feel the cool breeze against our faces as we went to the side of the house to pick up mangoes, oranges, guavas, or even avocadoes that had fallen from the trees. Sometimes Mom used a special rod that Grandpa made for her to help her pick the fruits she couldn't reach at the height of the tree. It was sometimes heartbreaking to watch Mom pick the pigeon peas and then sit and patiently shell the peas from their pods. She showed us how to plant roses, reminding us that a rose is precious and delicate like a child. With loving care and the right treatment, they can turn out to be beautiful roses; if not, they can wither and die. If the roses began to wither, we would have to start right back at square one and uproot the stem. The same goes for a child. If a child is neglected but then rescued on time, with lots of love, affection, and attention, that child can still become a productive, successful person. If the child is not rescued on time, he or she can wither and die. Our duties as kids were to water the plants early in the morning or when the sun went down. We soon had beautiful red, white, and yellow roses. Whatever Mom did, she did it with love and devotion. She taught us to have patience in everything we do, reminding us, "Rome wasn't built in a day."

There were many times I felt my heart would break whenever Mom fasted, especially during Holy Week. I didn't like seeing her lying there on the floor praying with tears streaming down her face, crying out to God. Most times, she only drank water. We would have to remain very quiet at all times; this was her special time with the Lord. We understood but were concerned for her health. If Mindy was down, she would always check to make sure Mom was all right. Mom wouldn't have anything to eat until she was through fasting. She would then have some olive oil to drink and then small portions of a well-balanced meal.

On Cindy's birthday, Mom always spent the day in prayer, asking God to guide and protect her at all times wherever she might be. Mom would say that with God's help we would see her soon one day. She taught us to say the rosary, the "Our Father," "I Believe in God," psalm 27, and the psalm 23. It was important for her that we say them on a regular basis.

Before Mom showed us how to wash clothes, she had to saw a large barrel in half, which was a very difficult task. She had to stop several times to wipe the sweat from her brow and catch her breath. When she was finally through, she would remove the upper half and wash the middle part thoroughly. She poured the water into the tub until it was almost filled. She placed the white clothes in first, then placed the scrubbing board inside the barrel and washed with the detergent. When she was through washing the white clothes, she would do the colored clothes. Mom would then spread the clothes to dry on the wire lines, which she attached to the trees at a height we could reach. I enjoyed attaching the clothes to the lines with clothespins, admiring the clothes swinging back and forth due to the heavy wind. Mom could tell when it was going to rain. The mountains looked gloomy, and the clouds looked dark. We had to rush outside to get the clothes off the line before the rain came pouring down. Whenever Mom had to iron, she would use the coal pot with charcoal. It was a painstaking procedure. She had to have the patience to get the coals to light evenly and then place the iron over the coals until it was hot. She carefully wiped underneath it and then ironed. When it was cool, she replaced it with another iron. If the coals burned out before she was done, she would have to add more coals until all the clothes were completely pressed. In order to keep the pleats smooth on my uniform, my mom showed me how to place it underneath my pillow. The following morning; my uniform looked like it had been ironed all over again.

Mom picked the cocoa from the tree and then cut them in half, took the seeds out from the pods, and then put it them in the sun. We would have to keep turning the seeds over until they were completely dried. Then Mom would patch and grind to make homemade cocoa. Growing up across the river was a warm experience that no one can ever take away from us. We will always continue to have beautiful memories of Mom while growing up across the river.

Whenever Mindy was off from work and wanted to go to the movies, and Mom told her she couldn't go because she needed Mindy home with us, I never saw her get an attitude. She understood the situation. Mitch and I would have a good laugh because we wanted her to stay with us instead of going out and have fun.

Shortly thereafter, she would return to Siparia. On one particular day, the weather forecast suddenly came as a newsflash, interrupting the regular programming and advising the public of the terrible storm that was about to hit the city. All residents living close to water were advised to evacuate immediately. Upon hearing the news, Mitch and I felt scared and asked Mom where we would go. She held us in her arms and said, "We have nowhere else to go. We have to trust in the Lord to protect us from whatever danger lays ahead of us." As the wind began to blow heavily, sending the fruits and vegetable trees in different directions, Mom got the plywood and began to nail down the windows.

Mom showed us how to use a hammer and nail so that when we were older, we could help. When she was through boarding up, she realized we didn't have enough vegetables inside the house. Mom made a bed for us on the floor and then placed us each in a crocus bag on the floor and told us not to move. With one hand holding a crow-cross bag (a brown bag with stitch holes and a string at the top to close the vegetables inside it) and the cutlass in the other hand, she headed for the garden to pick the fruits and vegetables. As we lay there side by side, we prayed for Mom's safety. We could hear the strong winds as they blew across the house. Mom made sure she picked all the ripe bananas, oranges, mangoes, and avocadoes. She finally came in, dropped the bag inside the kitchen, took another bag, and headed back out. With the winds blowing with a raging force, we were scared for Mom, but she told us to keep praying. On that particular day, God seemed to be waiting for Mom to complete her task. The strong winds kept throwing down all the fruit from off their trees. Mom was right there to pick them up before they were washed away. Finally, she finished. She took a rope and tied it around my waist, Mitch's waist, her waist, and the foot of the bed, as we continued praying.

The house began to shake as we lay there side by side. We fell asleep saying, "the Lord is my shepherd, I shall not want." When I awoke, I was on the bed, Mitch was playing the guitar, and Mom was praying at the altar, giving thanks and praise to the Lord for sparing our lives and the house. When she was through praying, she removed the boards that she had bolted down to keep the windows and doors safe. The yard was full of water, the fruit and vegetable trees had fallen down, and the river was overflowing. Inside, Mom always kept a large barrel with spring water, just in case the ravine should overflow, and she was right. We were surrounded by lots of water. The animals were all safe, including Rover. The neighbors from across the street came down to see if we were okay.

When the water finally calmed down, there were a lot of bamboo leaves, fruits, and branches on the ground. I asked Mom why she placed us in the crow-cross bag and tied us together. Mom calmly explained to me that if the house had fallen and washed us away into the river, we all would have been together. We would not have been separated. We learned on the news that several houses and properties were destroyed by the hurricane. We were one of the few blessed ones that survived the storm. If Mom hadn't gone out into the storm and picked the fruits and vegetables, we would not have had any because the water would have washed them away. When the water finally went down, there were no stones to walk over on. Mom had to gather several stones and place one on top of the other for us to cross over the river to attend school. The banana trees weren't washed away, but they collapsed. Mom had to prop up most of the fruit and vegetable trees. Mitch and I insisted on helping Mom clean the yard. It was too much for her alone. She told us what she wanted us to pull aside. She didn't want us pulling any heavy objects, especially me. Mom had to cut up the bamboo trees into small pieces. She also had to cut up the branches of the mango, guava, and orange trees so they could be manageable for us to handle. It was fun helping Mom do some of the chores. She made sure we had on our galoshes. When we were through helping her clean up the yard, we felt we could accomplish anything in life, regardless of how long or tough it may seem. Mom picked enough fruits and vegetables to last us awhile.

At night, whenever a stranger went into the garden to hunt for animals that only came out at night, Rover made sure we knew what was going on. Mom would open the window and turn on her flashlight to stop the intruders from going into the garden. However, sometimes they would ask her permission to hunt for the manicou. After shooting the animal, the hunters would show Mom what it looked like. They would have a feast with it and even offer some of it to the neighbors. There were always a lot of beautiful butterflies of different colors. We would admire how they flew around freely, resting on some of the flowers. They never seemed to be out of season. Whenever the lizards saw human beings, they would crawl fast under the cocoa tree or between the roses. Mom encountered a few scorpions, which she told us were dangerous. Mom was very brave; she would cut their heads off quickly. She explained that if the head is not cut off quickly, the poison from the scorpion could kill us. That is why it was important for her to wear her goulashes at all times when she stepped into the vegetable garden. Mom taught us to be brave and strong no matter what life throws at us.

chapter 7

Dad continued to send Mom clippings from the Trinidad newspaper that was sent to him in Curacao, insisting she visit the property that was on sale to build a house. Most times when Mom returned, she would be very upset because the location was only forest leading to nowhere. On another occasion when Dad sent more clippings for Mom to visit other properties, Mitch went with her. Upon their return, Mitch was very upset that Dad was sending Mom on a wild goose chase. Mitch and I sat down and wrote to Dad, letting him know that what he was doing to Mom was wrong. We went on to tell him what he could do with his money. We told him we were quite happy where we lived, until we could do better. He did not respond to our letters. Instead, he wrote to Mom and let her know that we were rude and disrespectful to him in our letters. We were forbidden to write to him unless Mom screened the letters. We had to apologize for being disrespectful. Regardless of who it was, we had to be respectful to our elders. Mom was not going to tolerate her children being rude or disrespectful to anyone. We had to express ourselves to him and let him know how much we were hurting. We understood he wanted us to have a better life, but with our aunts not visiting us, only God knew which one of them was sending the clippings for him.

Most absent fathers are not aware of the emotional pain they put their children through. They cannot see the void within their hearts, the look upon their faces as they wonder why he doesn't want to see them. At nights when we were tucked into bed and the lights were turned down low, Dad could not see the tears that streamed down our faces as we said a silent prayer to him. "Daddy, we are your children, Ellen and Mitch. Wherever you are, whatever you do, please remember us. Do not forsake your children. We love you." I never realized that somewhere around the world another child was saying a similar prayer to his dad. Not having our dad at home made our lives feel incomplete. Children should not blame themselves for their fathers not being in their lives. Remember that you are a special child of God, created for a reason and a special purpose. God has a special calling for you. Whatever path you choose in life, please let it be positive. Should you feel scared or alone, call out to God; reach out to him. Hold your Bible close to your heart and know he's right there beside you. Let him know how you feel and what you'd like him to do for you. Remember there's a difference between need and want. He will do what's in your best interest. Always keep in mind that nothing is impossible with the living God, the most high. Please give him a chance to be in your life and put him first in everything that you do. Let him be your guide. You'll be amazed at the wonderful things he can do for you. Should you doubt there's a God, take a look around you. Feel blessed to have the precious gift of sight, to be able to see the sun rise, your loved ones, the smile on a baby's face, or a butterfly. You have the opportunity to see what you're eating or drinking. You don't have to wonder what's in your meal. It's a beautiful thing to have the sense of smell, which enables you to smell flowers or freshly baked bread. You have the ability to hear your loved one's voice, the beautiful music on the radio, the birds whistling. It's the expression and reflection of God's love for you. You should not have any doubts. Should you ever feel tempted to follow the wrong crowd, look at yourself in the mirror, place your hand over your heart, and repeat these words: "I am a special child of God, and I will not let a few minutes of committing an illegal activity destroy me or my loved ones forever." Mom instilled this in us. It was our motto while growing up across the river. "I am a special person, a child of God, who can become anything I want to in life." It has helped us tremendously.

On a beautiful Saturday morning, Mom and I were looking out the window enjoying the scenery when one of the neighbors came charging into the avocadoes on the ground. In his hand was a large croc-cross bag and a cutlass. He looked up and saw us at the window. He then began to crush the avocadoes on the ground and said to Mom, "I have tried to kill you many times, but I didn't succeed. This time I will succeed." In a cool, calm, and collected tone, Mom said to him, "You kill my body, you don't kill my soul." I was scared and tugged at Mom for us to leave our home and run as far away as possible. Mom held me at arm's length and said to me, "My child, there's no reason to be afraid, and we have nowhere to run to. As long as we have God in our lives, he will protect and shield us from whatever evil awaits us." I asked Mom what he meant by saying those words, and Mom explained to me the best way she could. I turned to her and said, "It's a cruel world." Mom said, "It's a beautiful world in which we live. Yet there are some people who will go out of their way to hurt you. As long as you hold onto God's unchanging love, he will protect and shield us under his strong and loving arms. We cannot live in fear. We must have faith." I felt better but was still skeptical.

After his remarks to Mom, she paid closer attention to us. We were not allowed to wander off in the backyard; we had to be in the front at all times. Before leaving for school, Mom prayed with us, asking God to guide us and continue to protect us. She allowed us to wear our rosary around our necks instead of carrying it in our school bags. She wanted us to feel closer to God. Not long after Mr. Donald's remark to Mom, his daughter Susan came over and asked permission for me to play with her. We were the same age and attended the same school. Mom told us to play in the front yard. She was specific about us not going under the cocoa tree. Susan insisted on going. I reminded her of Mom's warning, but she did not listen. I ran after her to get her to come back into the yard. Instead, she climbed the cocoa tree like a squirrel; she was very fast.

I kept shouting for her to come down, but she didn't heed my warning. As I was about to go let Mom know what was happening, I heard a loud crashing sound. The branch broke, and Susan came crashing down with it. She was lying on the ground bleeding profusely. I ran home as fast as I could, screaming frantically. Mom got a few large bath towels and hydrogen peroxide and headed for the cocoa field. Susan was conscious but had lost a lot of blood. She also had a loose bowel. Mom was able to stabilize the bleeding. She told Mindy to call an ambulance and to get in touch with her parents. However, they were not at home. Instead of waiting for an ambulance, Mom carefully picked her up and took her to the hospital in a cab. Mindy left a note for Susan's parents, notifying them of the incident.

Susan had emergency surgery to remove the object that had pierced her front and back and also to repair the physical damage. Mom stayed at the hospital until the surgery was over and waited until Susan regained consciousness. She returned home several hours later, exhausted. Susan's parents came the following morning to thank Mom for being there for their child. They said they had returned home very late that night and could not have gone to the hospital. Mr. Donald became humble toward Mom after learning of the seriousness of Susan's condition. He apologized to Mom for what he had previously said to her. She needed to know why he said it. He said he envied all the fruits and vegetables she had, while he was struggling to make ends meet to feed his family. Mom responded by letting him know it came with hard work and will power. She had no one to help her except God. If he needed any fruits or vegetables, all he had to do was ask her. There was absolutely no need for him to threaten her. He said he had too much pride to ask her for anything. Under the watchful eye of us, Mom went into the garden with Mr. Donald and his wife and gave them several fruits and vegetables in a large croc-cross bag. Later on that night after dinner, I asked Mom why she helped Susan, knowing what her father had said to her. Mom said that every child is precious and innocent. She went on to let me know you have to have clean hands and a pure heart to enter the kingdom of heaven.

Not long after the incident with Susan, her brother, Mike, went and climbed the mango tree without asking Mom's permission. The next thing we heard was loud screams coming from under the mango tree. We looked out into the yard and saw Mike running toward the house, screaming and holding his right eye. He told Mom that a snake had stung him in the eye. With Mom's nursing experience, she knew what to do to help prevent any infection. Mom took him to the hospital because his parents were not at home. Even though he was twenty-one, Mom would not allow him to go the hospital alone.

The doctors were able to save his eyesight. The doctors credited Mom for what she did to help prevent any further infection or the loss of the eye. From then on, their parents were very cordial toward Mom. Mr. Donald would humble himself to ask Mom for fruits or vegetables whenever he needed to feed his family. She gave him what he needed wholeheartedly. After that experience, Mom warned us to never threaten to hurt anyone, physically, spiritually, or otherwise, because the hole you dig for that innocent person will really be for you or your loved ones. We learned that your own children can fall into the trap you set for someone else. Mom still found the time to visit them at the hospital. When their parents couldn't afford to visit them, Mom would give them the money.

Mom always kept an emergency kit at home containing cotton wool, Dettol, hydrogen peroxide, and other antibiotics just in case there was an emergency. She also made sure she kept our appointments to see the pediatrician and the specialist.

chapter 8

Uncle Randolph, the cardiologist residing in London, came to visit Mom during his vacation. He was concerned that Mom still did not have any contact with her other child, Cindy. Mom collapsed into his arms and poured her heart out to him in regards to Cindy, her second child that was kidnapped by her father. Cindy's dad had absolutely no intention of allowing her to return to Mom, even though at the time, he was gravely ill. Uncle Randolph went to Grenada in search of Cindy. He was determined to bring her back to her mother, and he sure did. It was a joyous moment for mother and child. At sixteen, she was a gracious young lady with beautiful grey eyes. She seemed lonely and was the spitting image of Mom. Mom had her work cut out for her. We were introduced to her as her brother and sister. Mindy had already known her. It was an emotional reunion. The tears, the hugs, and the kisses never seemed to stop. There was no turning back. Mom would take long walks with her to show her the beautiful rose garden. She would pick a rose and stick it in her pretty black hair as Mom continued to show her how she planted the fruits and vegetables. Cindy seemed to be impressed. Mom would spend hours talking to her in private about the birds and the bees. She was trying to make up for lost time.

Cindy later said she often wondered why she was treated differently from her other siblings. They wore shoes and socks to attend school, and she had to walk barefooted. Her brothers and sisters would be dropped off in front of their school, and she would have to walk over a mile to get to her school. Our hearts went out to her. We wanted to protect her in every way we could. She was very intellectual and won a scholarship to attend a prestigious high school. Uncle Randolph's gift to her was a box of pens and pencils, which she cherished. She was very good at French, Spanish, and English. We enjoyed listening to her translate English into Spanish and French into English. We were very proud of her. Mitch and Cindy enjoyed conversing about the languages they were being taught at school. Whenever they had exams, they would be up late at night, studying by the lamp. They were born the same month, and had the same horoscope.

At nights after dinner, we all knelt down to say our prayers, but Cindy didn't know how to pray. Mom had to teach her. We would take turns praising the Lord, giving him our testimony. Uncle Randolph and Mom were very upset to learn of the emotional and psychological abuse she suffered at the hands of those responsible for caring for her. Shortly thereafter, word came to Mom that Cindy's father was dying and he asked her to forgive him for the pain he caused her. The emotional healing slowly began. Sometimes Cindy made us laugh with her silly jokes. There was a story she told us about the student who couldn't spell "uncle." The teacher told her she would have to remain after school to write the word several times until she got it right. Upon seeing her uncle, she asked him, in the presence of the teacher, "You ain't see Elli?" The teacher said to her, "You can spell the word uncle, and you said you couldn't." The student was unaware her sentence sounded as though she had spelled the word uncle. She was asking her uncle if he had seen her friend Elle. We found it to be very funny. The other joke I remembered was about a patient. Her physician was concerned about her low blood count. He advised her to get a "bottle of beef iron and wine tonic." Instead, on her way home, she bought a pound of beef and a bottle of wine. When she went home, she cooked the beef, and while ironing, she drank the wine and began to whine. When she returned to the doctor, she told him she did as he had instructed her to do and she felt much better. She then told him what she did. He had to give her a prescription to have filled. We all had a hearty laugh at this joke. Both Cindy and Mitch were doing very well at school. Mom was pleased with their report cards.

When I was fifteen, Mom gave me consent to join the Legion of Mary. Young people from the Roman Catholic faith attended meetings once a week to learn more of the powerful word of God. We were invited to attend conferences to meet other members from around the country. It also gave us the opportunity to meet other young people who were seriously considering entering the convent or the monastery. It was a wonderful experience for me. It was at one of those meetings that I met my very good friends. I believe faith brought us together. Martha, Asia, and I were members of the Legion of Mary. We all met while attending a conference for young Christians. They never looked down on me because of where I lived; we all enjoyed each other's company and took turns visiting each other's family. Both their parents lived together. There were so many interesting things to talk and learn about. Asia and I wanted to enter the convent. Martha wanted to become a nurse. Asia wanted Mom's opinion about her entering the convent. She said she felt comfortable talking to Mom instead of her mother. Mom advised her it was a decision she had to be very sure of. It wasn't fun and games. Once she entered the convent, there would be no turning back. She had to be sure she wanted to serve God for the rest of her life. Not long after the discussion with Mom, Asia brought her fiancé to meet Mom. She became a teacher and later got married.

They enjoyed the cool breeze at my home and admired the beautiful fish in the river. Sometimes they would take their shoes off and step into the water and prance around like little kids. They admired the beautiful roses, fruits, and vegetables. They often said they wished they were living with me instead of living in the city. We kept in touch on a regular basis. With Mom's consent, we made arrangements to meet. If something came up before the planned event, I would call them or they would write to me. Those were the good old days.

One day when I returned from school, Mom had a visitor. She introduced us to Clara. She told us she was the ex-babysitter of one of our sisters back in the day. She was pregnant. Her boyfriend had moved to England. She had not heard from him and had nowhere to go. She asked Mom if she could stay with her for a while until she found a place. After discussing it with us in private, Mom wanted our opinion. I told Mom I didn't feel comfortable with her staying in our home but it was up to her. Mitch didn't object, and the others agreed with her staying. After all, she was once their babysitter. When I returned from school, she had arrived with her personal belongings. She and my sisters were enjoying the beautiful view overlooking the river. As soon as I walked in, she said, "Good evening," and then looked into my eyes and said, "You see Ellen, she will not turn out to be anything good in life. She'll have eleven bastards and will not know who the fathers are." Stunned and scared, I just stood there wishing Mom was there to rescue me. My sisters, who are much older than I am, did not tell her it was wrong of her to say those things. Instead they all had a good laugh at my expense. As I stood there feeling sorry for myself, Mom suddenly opened her bedroom door and ushered me in. Mom then let Clara have it. She told her she was pregnant and had nowhere to go, and Mom was depriving her children for Clara to have somewhere to sleep, and this is what she said to me, knowing I was hard of hearing. Mom told Clara to start looking for another place to live. She told her she wanted her out of her home as soon as possible. She made her understand that this was the home Ellen's father was helping to provide for her, and she scolded my sisters for laughing at me. She then returned to the bedroom and with a switch, she let me have it. Mom wanted me to remember that I was a special child of God, and that I will someday become somebody in life. I had to keep repeating those words after her. "I will not have eleven bastards and not know who the fathers are." When Mom was through, we both cried. She wanted me to always remember those words. *I am somebody special and I will not have eleven bastards and not know who the fathers are.*

From that day on, I disliked Clara and couldn't wait for her to leave our home. I began to observe my sisters more closely. Both my sisters felt powerful with Clara staying there. They didn't seem to respect Mom as much anymore, especially Mindy. I realized she was showing her true colors more and more every day toward Mom, and I couldn't wait for them all to leave. Whenever Mitch and I did something wrong, Mindy wouldn't tell Mom it was both of us that did the mischief; instead she would always say I did it. Mom finally got the message. Throughout my adult years, I have kept those words in the back off my head. I say to the parents who may be helping their friends by letting them stay at your home, observe your children carefully, making sure they are not being verbally or emotionally abused.

To the children whose parents have finally found them, please don't hold any animosity in your heart toward your parents. Their lives didn't seem complete until they found you. I'm sure their lives were never the same since you were taken from their arms. Don't try to hurt your siblings in any way. Please be aware that your siblings, upon learning they had a lost sibling out there, also suffered in silence. Don't hold it against them. I strongly urge you to find peace, love, and unity in your heart. It's not every day we are given a second chance with our family. You don't need any regrets. It's not going to be easy, but you can do it with the strength and help of God, mediating, and also by listening to songs of inspiration. Embrace them with love. Reach out and thank God for his wonderful blessings. In time, the void will be filled. Please avoid doing anything stupid or cruel to get back at your parents. Please don't do it; you will regret it. Remember a higher power is watching your every move. If you make the wrong move, in the stillness of the night when you least expect it, he'll take it from there. You certainly don't want that.

chapter 9

At sixteen, while cleaning the rose garden, I tried pulling up one of the toughest weeds, known as sweet broom, when I suddenly jerked back. I felt a sharp pain in my ear. It hurt for a few minutes, but I continued to clean the garden until I completed it. I did not think it was necessary to mention anything to Mom. The following morning when I awoke, I felt a lancing pain above my ear. I told Mom how I felt and what had happened the day before. When she examined me, there was an abscess above my ear, and my temples were swollen. Mom immediately rushed me to the emergency room. When we arrived there, being Saturday, it was very crowded. We had no idea when I would be seen by a doctor. I began to groan and moan in pain, and Mom went to talk to the nurse. Shortly after speaking to her, I was seen by the attending physician, who admitted me to the ear, noise, and throat ward. I was given two aspirin tablets and told I would have to wait until the Monday to see my ear, nose, and throat specialist. Mom was allowed to remain with me past the visiting time. I felt scared and was in excruciating pain. In the stillness of the night, I paced the floor, wishing the pain would go away, but it never did. As I stood on the terrace, I could see the nurses walking bravely toward the nurses' hostel after their night shift. The pain was unimaginable. I felt weak and was not sure I was going to survive until Monday. I kept praying and wishing for a miracle. As I walked back toward my bed, I looked around and admired the other patients as they slept so peacefully.

Back then, it was an open ward. The girls were on one side, and the minor boys were much lower down on the same floor. A large curtain was drawn, separating us. There were no private rooms. Whenever the nurse had to take a patient's temperature or they had to be washed, they would be screened and then removed. Only the seriously ill patients were screened entirely. The following day, while standing on the terrace, trying to deal with the pain, another patient, Claire, joined me. One of the nurses came over and joined our conversation. Claire was fourteen, and the nurse told her she was too young to be sexually active. Claire asked the nurse how she knew. She replied, "We are trained to know these things." Claire turned to me and asked the nurse, "How about her?" Here I was in excruciating pain and had not even started talking to boys yet, and there she was asking the nurse about me. The nurse said, "She's not into anything yet."

When Dr. Lee Young walked into the room on Monday and saw the abscess above my ear and realized how much pain I was in, he and the nurse escorted me to the examination room. When he was through examining me, he requested to have two more nurses. As I sat on the examination bed, I wondered why he needed more nurses. He then took a surgical knife from the container containing the sterilized instruments, placed it through the burning lamp, cleaned it with rubbing alcohol, held it up, and walked toward me with his headlight on above his forehead. I asked him what he was going to do. He said nothing and told me to lie down. To him, time was crucial. The nurses held me down tightly as I tried to struggle from underneath their grip. I felt the sharp pain above my ear, and I felt my eye balls protruding from my head. I began to groan louder and louder. He was cruel, and this was inhumane. Dr. Lee Young rocked the knife into me. When it was finally over, he began to squeeze the blood from my temples. The pain was excruciating. He had no mercy on me. I felt it was the end. The pain was too much to bear. As I lay on my side, words cannot express the sharp physical pain

I endured. I eventually found the physical strength to ask him why he couldn't have put me under anesthesia. He said there wasn't much time; the inflammation was going up to my brain.

When I looked at the blood, I was devastated; the blood was not red, but black. I was given two more aspirins. The wound was cleaned and dressed, and I was escorted back to my room. During the course of the day, I was examined by an ophthalmologist. He wanted to be sure I could see. However, five years later, it was imperative for me to wear corrective lenses, which I learned I should have been wearing since after the mastoid surgery because my eyes were badly strained. Mom and the rest of the family came to visit me later that day. During their visit, the nurse came into my room and took my temperature. The family was asked to step out, and Mom asked what was wrong. The nurse told her I had a high temperature. The nurse screened me around and then rubbed me down with rubbing alcohol. Several minutes later, my temperature was back to normal.

Mom was later told I was going to have major surgery the following day, and she was asked to sign the necessary documents. Before doing so, Mom had a lot of questions to ask. The inflammation had gone up to my brain, and hopefully they could correct the problem of me being hard of hearing. Only my Mom was aware that I had learned to read lips. By doing so, I didn't have to have questions repeated to me over and over, or have people speak loudly to me. Mom and I learned the brain specialist who was going to do the surgery was no other than Dr. Mohammed. We had been turned away again and again, and here we were in an emergency crisis, and he would be the one doing the surgery. I wondered where was he throughout the years when we travelled for so many miles to see him with a referral from my pediatrician. The damage was already done now, and there were no guarantees that I was going to come through alive. I thought of the blows the bullies kept giving me at the back of my head and also the pulling of my ear that had been infected. I felt my life was going to be over; nothing mattered anymore. The facts were laid on the table for Mom and me. We were told Dr.

Mohammed was the best in the country and I was going to be in safe hands. It didn't give me much comfort. As I sat there listening to the doctors talk to Mom, my thoughts began to wander of. I was beginning to have excruciating pain all over again. I thought of Daddy. I could barely remember him, and now I may never get a chance to see him and let him know how much I love him. I also thought that I may never get to enter the convent to serve God, but there was nothing I could do. I had to accept what was about to happen.

When visiting hours were over, Mom didn't want to leave, and I sure didn't want her to leave me. She held me close to her heart and began to pray for me to have a safe and successful surgery, leaving my life in the hands of the Lord. She wanted me to trust in him. I had no other choice but to trust in God. Mom was allowed to stay with me until late that night. She was right there when the sign was placed above my bed, instructing the nurses who were about to change shifts what was about to happen and that I was not allowed to have anything to eat or drink after a certain hour. Mom left late. She promised to be back, stating she'd be right there when I returned from surgery. She looked exhausted. It reminded me of the day when she learned that Lenny was going to die. I had to get sufficient rest; it was going to be a long day. The nurses were back and forth to check on me as I tried to hide under the covers, too scared to look up.

The following morning at 7:00 a.m., Billy, the ward attendant, came in to shave my hair. When he was through shaving three quarters of my hair off, he needed to shave my arms and legs. I asked him why, and he explained that they may have to do a skin graft and he was not sure what part of my body the doctor would need it from. The children who were schedule to have their tonsils and adenoids (the tissues in the nostrils) removed were sent home. Their surgery had to be rescheduled. Before going in for surgery, I asked Billy to give my handkerchief to my mom for me just in case I didn't make it through surgery. He promised he would. Before going home, most of the children gathered around the stretcher to wish me well, promising to see me soon. It made me feel a little better that they cared. It was a very tense moment as we took the elevator down to the operating room. Mr. Billy kept reassuring me that everything was going to be all right.

When we got there, Dr. Mohammed was sitting on a table with his legs crossed. He was praying. Mr. Billy told him the patient was ready. Dr. Mohammed was not only the top brain specialist, he was also known to be able to predict the outcome of his patients' surgery. He opened his eyes and said to me, "It's going to be a rough road ahead, but you'll eventually pull through." I didn't ask him what he meant. I was in a lot of pain. I remember there was this particular nurse with a warm smile and kind eyes, who kept reassuring me not to be scared as she held my hand. She promised she was going to be right there with me throughout the surgery. She made me feel a bit relaxed. I was told that the very tall doctor standing at my bedside was going to be my anesthesiologist. I felt the sharp needle piercing my arm. I was then asked to count backwards. I fell into a deep sleep.

I remember hearing my aunt's voice very clearly asking someone what he was doing here. The gentleman replied, "This is the patient I told you about. She asked me to give her handkerchief to her mom if she didn't make it." He then asked her what she was doing there, and she replied, "This is my niece." My Aunt Lolita told Mom that Billy was her neighbor. I recognized my mom's voice telling them it was a coincidence. I heard Dr. Shaw remove the screen door and close it, telling my family they had to step outside. I felt the sharp, stinging pain on my arm as he began to slap me. He continued calling out my name, telling me it was time to wake up. I wanted desperately to scream at him to let him know he was hurting me, but the words wouldn't come out. I heard the cranking of the bed handle as it began to rise; it felt like I was being raised to heaven. My head felt very heavy. I heard everything that was being said, and there was no need for anyone to speak so loudly. I could hear, smell, and feel, but I couldn't see, move, or respond to anything or anyone. I then heard Dr. Shaw ask my mom if she knew what I wanted most out of life. My mom said I wanted to see my dad. He asked her where was he, and she told him in Curacao. He asked her how soon she could get him there, explaining, "We have to get him here as soon as possible because we are losing her." Mom cried out, "Oh God, no! Jesus, Mary, and Joseph, help me." He went on tell her that Dr. Mohammed discovered inflammation in my brain. There was a lot that had to be done. I was given a skin graft to my ear, which had to be taken from my right arm. I had lost a lot of blood, and they had finally found my blood type, which was rare. Dr. Shaw went on to let Mom know my condition was critical. He kept repeating the same question over and over. How soon could she get my father there? Poor Mom; she didn't have the answer. He said to her there was not much time.

I felt very weak. I wanted desperately to say to them, "Guys, I'm here. I'm alive. I can hear you, I just can't move, see, or respond to you." The doctor needed to know if there was anything he could do, and Mom said no. He then told her if she needed anything, not to hesitate to ask the nurse. Dr. Shaw wanted to help Mom as much as he could. He realized the seriousness of my condition. If only I had been seen by Dr. Mohammed back when I was supposed to, my condition would not have deteriorated. I learned at an early age that there is a code of silence among doctors. Even though they are aware that their colleague is doing wrong, they will not report it. Instead they argue among themselves and watch the doctor's back, while the patient is left to suffer in silence. I wondered if Daddy would have taken the matter seriously. Mom was crying hysterically. Dr. Shaw tried his best to comfort her, letting her know they had to do a lot of praying. He even told her that at sixteen I had my whole life ahead of me and I had a lot to give to the world. Mom said she knew that. I often wondered what he meant by those words. Dr. Shaw realized that even though Mom was poor, she was educated and he had to be straightforward with her. Even though Mom sounded very upset, she was also very angry. I could hear it in her voice. It was because of the many disappointments and insults she had to endure, and because we never saw Dr. Mohammed until this crucial point of my life. Dr.

Shaw said he understood and tried to calm Mom down while she cried uncontrollably. I wished they didn't talk so loudly. If only they knew I could hear every word that was being said. The conversation started to bother me. Hearing about my condition made me feel terrible, and there was nothing I could do about it. I kept hearing the screen being pulled backed and forth. I believed it was the nurses checking my vital signs. The only way I can describe being semi-conscious is "floating in a hole of darkness," which comes with different stages of wanting desperately to rise above the surface.

I heard Mom's soft voice and felt her gentle touch when she said to me, "It is 5:00 in the morning." She said it was Wednesday, the day after I had the surgery. She went on to tell me she had gotten in touch with Dad and he was coming. As Mom continued to talk to me, she gently massaged my head. Even though three-quarters of my head was bandaged, I could feel her warm and gentle touch. I felt safe and secure. I felt myself rising to a higher stage from a zero to maybe stage three. Mom sounded confident. I wanted desperately to rise above the surface but couldn't. My life was in God's hands. I felt helpless. I wanted very much to see and talk to Mom, but I couldn't move a muscle. Just knowing she was right there with me made me feel so very safe. I hung on to her every word. I believe Mom knew I was skeptical and could hear her. She began to sound more convincing. I wanted to ask her so many questions, but the words just couldn't come out. I learned that when there is a close bond between a mother and a child, especially in a life and death situation, it's so powerful that even if the child cannot physically communicate, the mom tends to know what her child is thinking. Mom seemed to know the questions I needed to ask her without asking her. What was Daddy travelling by? How long would it take him to get there? How long would he stay? Would he reject me because I would not be able to see or respond to him? Would he walk away after seeing me with my head in bandages? Would he still love me for who I am? Mom answered every question without me uttering a word. She said Dad was coming by ship because he was afraid of flying.

She went on to tell me the ship would take a while to get to Trinidad because it had to stop off at different ports. He would be staying for a long time to be with his daughter and to see her enter the convent. Dad would always love me unconditionally. He knew I had major surgery and was very proud of me for being so brave, and he was happy to know I was alive. He would always love me for who I am, and nothing could ever change that. Just knowing Mom was right there at my side gently talking to me, holding my hand, made me wish I could have gotten better quickly.

I had to arise above the surface. I couldn't continue to lie in a hole of darkness. I needed God to help me. I didn't want my dad to see me like that. Most of my beautiful hair was gone. When Mom was through talking to me, there was a pause and then sobs. Oh, how I wished I could put my arms around her and let her know I could hear her and everything was going to be all right. I realized how devastating it must have been for her, talking to me all that time and unaware I could hear her every word. I wanted Mom to know I was going to be all right, that it was only a matter of time. Only God had the answer. In the midst of her sobbing, she stopped, blew her nose, and said to me, "I know you can hear me. I can feel it. Just hold on and be strong." I wanted to smile but couldn't. She silently heard me. I looked forward to her many visits ahead and the news she would have for me in regards to Daddy. I was not interested in hearing anything else except what port the ship was at.

I could hear Dr. Shaw's loud footstep as he pulled the screen wide open and then closed it. He must have seen the change in my physical appearance because he said I looked rested. I believe he and some of the nurses knew I could hear them. Nurse Rogers would speak to me as though she knew I could hear her, even though I could not respond. Whenever they opened the screen door and walked in, they would let me know who they were and what procedure they were going to do. Mom always came to see me early in the morning. She would gently place her hand on my forehead and pray for me. As she gently massaged my head, she reminded me how much she loved and missed me and how she liked that I showed her love openly. I was not afraid to let her know how much I loved her while the others kept their feelings buckled up inside. She reminded me I was a special child of God.

I deeply wanted to thank Mom for not scorning me when I couldn't hear her and for having the patience to administer the ear drops every day and make sure the cotton wool was properly placed in my ear before I left for school. That was one of the reasons the bullies called me deafy. Mom was never impatient with me; she didn't scream or yell at me. She knew how much I wanted to succeed in life, but I was always told I had to avoid studying too much because I would put too much pressure on my brain.

Mom found the time to visit me again in the evening. She always told me what day and time it was but not the month or year. I learned later on that it was important not to let your loved one know the month or the year in which they are semi-conscious. It can set back their recovery. At some point one day, I heard the door slide open. Someone walked in but didn't say anything. I wanted to ask who was there, but the words wouldn't come out. I then heard Mitch say, "You've got a lot of bandages on your head. I didn't know it was that bad." At fourteen, he had just returned from school. Instead of going home, he stopped by to visit me. He said he had to come to see me before returning home. I heard him open my cupboard, and then he went on to let me know he was hungry and was having one of my bananas, cracking a joke and telling me he wished I could have one with him. He said he hoped and prayed I would wake up soon. He wanted me to know how much he missed me. I wanted to tell him I missed him too but couldn't. He told me what subjects he did that day at school, which sounded interesting. I admired Mitch very much. He not only sounded intelligent, but also like a leader.

Mindy left her job so she could be there for Mom and the rest of the family. When Mom couldn't visit me, Mindy would come early in the morning. She would let me know Mom had taken the time to tend to the fruits and vegetables in the garden before the sun got too hot. I could hear her asking me how was I doing. I wanted to respond to her question by letting her know I wanted to come out from the hole of darkness but I couldn't. She would let me know Mom sent me bananas and oranges from the garden. I could hear her say my cousin Marvin also sent orange juice from the factory where he worked, and he also sent his best wishes. He could not bear to see me in that condition. She went on to say the nurse would have to keep the orange juices in the refrigerator because she didn't know how long I would be in the hospital.

Mom finally came to see me more often, letting me know her work in the garden was completed. In times of trouble, just hearing your mom's voice can lift your spirit and bring you back from the depth of no return. Dr. Shaw walked in with his brisk demeanor and said to me, "Ellen, I'm going to change your dressing." He said he would try to be gentle as possible. I could hear him talking to the nurses, asking them for what he needed. As soon as he was through taking the bandage off my head, I heard one of the nurses say that there was so much blood on the bandage. As he started to remove the dressing from the back of my ear, it felt like my skull was about to explode. I began to get dizzy. I wished he would have stopped the procedure. I wanted to scream out in pain, but I couldn't. I felt I wasn't going to pull through. The pain had taken me into a whole new direction. Dr. Shaw tried his best to go easy on me but was unaware of how much pain I was in or how I felt. It was horrible, but how could he have known? When he was finally through redressing my head, I heard him say to me, "Ellen, if you can hear me, I want you to squeeze my hand." I wanted to but couldn't move. He repeated the question. I still couldn't move a muscle. He then instructed the nurse on what the next procedure was. He sounded disappointed that I couldn't follow his instructions. I felt like I was in la-la land, a place of no return. My stage level seemed to have dropped low.

The only time I saw any light in the hole of darkness was when he was through dressing my ear. I had this dream that I was holding my brother's right hand and an angel's left hand. There were two other angels, and we were floating under the bright blue sky. It was beautiful. The sun had set, and the pale blue and white clouds just lay still as we floated underneath the beautiful sky. Each time I tried to bring myself up to be at the same level with my brother, he would push me back down. I felt sad that my brother didn't want me to be with him. After three attempts, he finally said to me, "You have to go back, it's not time yet."

I kept hearing the screen sliding back and forth. There seemed to be lot of movement. I could tell I was slipping away and the doctors and nurses knew it. I kept hearing their whispers, "We have to get the family here as soon as possible." My life was over. I could still hear but was very weak. I could not move, see, or respond.

The pain was unbearable. I wished Mom was there, and I was scared. I wanted to rise above the surface into the sunlight, and it was impossible. I believed God knew how desperately I wanted to rise from the hole of darkness above the surface into the sunlight to feel the cool breeze against my face, to see the sun and the beauty of the sky. I was in another dimension, and only God could bring me back from that hole of darkness. My life was in his hands. It felt like I was hanging on by a piece of thread. It was only matter of time before my life was completely over. I didn't want to hear about Dad any more.

I heard Cindy's voice. She had returned from work and stopped by. I remembered her letting me know that even though she didn't know she had other siblings, I made her feel happy. I was happy to learn of this. Mom joined Cindy at my bedside. I continued to hear the loud voices of children talking and whimpering, but no one seemed to be making much sense. I then heard Cindy say, "You're giving her the final rite?" And then I heard Father Michael say, "Yes I am." I heard Mom begin to sob. I wanted desperately to say, "Hi, guys! I'm here. I'm alive. What are you doing? Can you not see me? I can hear you. I just can't see or respond to you." I heard the priest say his prayers. The others in the room joined in. I felt the cold water on my face and on my arms. Mom, Mindy, Cindy, and the others in the room were sobbing and praying.

When they were through praying, I heard the nurse come in and say, "Everybody cannot remain in the room together. It has to be one at a time to say your good-byes."

Nothing seemed right anymore. I recognized the voice of one of the members from the Legion of Mary. She told me my mom had told them I was sick at the hospital and they all wanted to see me. They were there with their supervisor. Each one that came in told me how much they missed me attending the meetings. I even recognized my friends' voices. They were allowed to come into my room together. They were sobbing loudly. Oh I wished they didn't; it was affecting my spirit. I couldn't put my arms around them and let them know I was alive. They wanted me to get better soon so we could all spend as much time together as possible. It sounded good and I sure wanted that very much. But how could I? I felt the warmth of each of their hands as they told me which of their hands was holding mine. Martha was holding my left hand, and Asia was holding my right hand as they prayed for me. Asia was good at praying. Her words sounded powerful. When they were through praying, they gently massaged my hands and continued to talk to me, insisting I had to get better soon. In between, I could hear the sniffling; they were crying but were trying not to be loud. It was time for them to leave. I wished they didn't have to.

The following morning when Mom came in to see me, she told me the day and time, letting me know it was the following day, after I received the final rite. Hearing Mom's soothing voice made me feel very safe. She let me know Dad's ship was nearing port. She then placed her hand on my forehead and began to pray, asking God to heal her child, to raise her back up from the dead as he raised Lazarus back to life. As she continued to pray, I felt her hand begin to shake. Mom was getting the manifestation. When she was through, she told me she was going to stay with me throughout the night to ensure everything was going to be all right. At some point, I heard the chair move closer to my bed. Mom let me know she had just moved the chair closer to my bed so she could hold my hand. My stage level must have gone up because I could feel myself moving to a higher level, wanting very much to rise above the darkness.

Throughout the night, I could hear the screen moving back and forth. Mom would let me know the nurse was checking the machine to be sure it was working. Mom let me know it was the following morning then, and she would be helping the nurse sponge me. If Mom only knew how safe I felt hearing her voice and knowing she was right there beside me. When they were through sponging me, I heard Mom tell the nurse she'd dress me. She told the nurse she preferred if the dressing wasn't changed that day. Mom seemed to know how excruciating it was for me whenever the bandages were changed. Mom wanted me to know how much she loved me and wanted me to get better soon. She would say, "You got to help me too, Ellen. I cannot do this alone. God and his archangels are here and they do want you to get better. Just look forward to seeing your dad. You both have a lot of catching up to do." With Mom and God's help, I could certainly rise above the darkness and into the sunlight.

It was time for her to leave. After spending days with me, I believed I could get better. Before leaving, she said she would be back later that day. She needed to get some rest and prepare for Dad's arrival. She wanted me to remain strong and look forward to Dad's arrival. Later that day, I didn't hear Mom's voice. I heard the rest of the family letting me know how much they cared. Cindy and Mitch were at my bedside. They talked about what subjects he did at school. I wished I could have joined in their conversation, but I couldn't. I could only listen to them conversing. Their subject changed to me as they pondered my fate. They wondered whether I would live or die and how long it would be before they knew. I wanted desperately to say, "I'm here in spirit and I can hear your every word."

I don't know how long it was, but one night I opened my eyes and saw a young boy standing by my bed, staring down at me. He wanted to know why I was sleeping all the time. I wanted to answer him, but the words would not come out. He told me his name and wanted to know mine. He continued to ask me why I was not answering him. He further told me he was the son of Bernard, a radio personality we knew very well. Every Sunday evening, he had a show for children on the air, along with a female colleague. He said he had returned to have his tonsils removed. Unfortunately, he was one of the children that had to leave because I had to have major surgery. He was about nine years old. When he realized I was not responding to his questions, he began to shout, "Nurse! Nurse! She's awake! Her eyes are open!" I'm not sure why, but I found my eyes closed again. I'm not sure if it was due to shock. The nurse came toward the screen door and told him to get back into bed because he had surgery in the morning. Then she told him he had no right to be in my room. When she came in, I heard her movements. Then she stepped back into the ward and told David he was wrong. He insisted he had seen me with my eyes wide open. I found my eyes closed and was unable to open them again.

I continued to hear my loved ones praying over me. They were not too loud; this was very good. They told me of all the good things that were happening, including how well Mitch was doing at school. Mindy had completed her studies in shorthand and typing. My best friends, Martha and Asia, came again to visit me, reminding me of the good times we all had together at the park and how much they enjoyed my peanut punch. They let me know how much they missed me and wanted me to get better. They would pause. Did someone stop them from talking? Then it would be the crying sound. Asia was much more emotional. Sobbing, she would say she couldn't stand to see me lying down like that. She begged, "Ellen, please wake up, for our sake, for your mom, and also for your dad. He's on his way. He's not far away." I felt like I was moving to a higher stage; my dad was not far away. I had to get better and rise above the surface into the sunlight. How could I? My life was still in God's hands. He had to know how much I wanted this. I heard the bell ring; visiting hours were over. They both began to sob. They said they didn't want to leave. I heard the screen door open, and the nurse told them they could remain five more minutes but that they shouldn't sob too loud. "It's not good for her to hear you all like this." Soon after, it was time to say good-bye. I felt their kisses.

I heard the screen door screech open loudly, and then there was a pause. Lying in a hole of darkness can be scary when you are unable to see who's entering your room. You can only wait to hear what the individual is saying to you. I heard a female with a loud husky voice say to me, "It's time to rise and shine. Why are you still sleeping? At sixteen years old, you have the whole world ahead of you." I could not believe what she had said. Who was she? And why was she talking to me in this manner? She went on to tell me she had been transferred to this ward and was there to "snap me out of shock." She was talking to me as if I could respond to her. She wanted to know what was holding me back from waking up. I wished she didn't speak so loudly; if only she knew how her loud voice was affecting my spirit. Who did she think she was? She further stated that my dad had arrived at the port and it was time to rise and shine to greet him. I felt my stage level rising up and down like a scale. I felt upset but couldn't cry. Why was she doing that to me? She said my dad had arrived. He would put her in her place for talking to me like that when I could not even see, much less respond to her. After giving me a good tongue lashing, she opened the screen door and closed it loudly. I wished I could tell her off. I felt my stage level go down very low. I didn't want to see Dad anymore. That nurse was cruel and mean. Mom finally came in later that same day. She told me that the other patients told her what they overheard the nurse say to me. She wanted to give her a piece of her mind, but she had already left early. She said she was going to remain with me for a few days. I felt even safer. She continued to tell me of all the good news that was happening at home. I could smell the scent of roses, but where was the scent coming from? It seemed to be in my room. Mom said she brought me some red and white roses from the garden. Then she went on to let me know the neighbors had sent their best regards and wishes to me. Next thing I knew, Mom told me it was her second day there. After sponging me off and getting me dressed in the nightgown she bought for me, she told me how lovely it was on me.

The day finally came when I suddenly opened my eyes and smiled at my mom. She burst out with, "Thank you, Jesus, for saving my child's life! Thank you, God!" The medical residents who were about to make their rounds with their senior doctor heard my mom's loud cry to God. They all rushed in along with the nurses, checking my vital signs, asking me to take a deep breath in and out, to squeeze their hands, and repeat their words. They wanted me to say my name and address. They were acting like I was from a different planet. I could not wait for them to leave so that I could ask Mom the burning question that helped keep me afloat. When the doctors were through examining me and left the room, I finally asked, "Where's Daddy?" Mom cleared her throat and said he was resting at home after a long journey. I could not wait to get home. However, I could not leave right away. I had to have several tests done to be sure I was well enough to return home.

When I asked Mom for Dad, she said, "I knew you heard me all along." I asked her how she knew. She replied, "A mother's instincts are very powerful where her child is concerned." She even told me of the questions she knew I wanted to ask her. She was so very right. It was an emotional day for Mom and me when I finally opened my eyes and asked her for Dad. She cried uncontrollably. Everything around me looked so very different. I had to touch Mom's face and her hand to be sure I was not dreaming. Mom told me I was semiconscious for six months.

The day finally came for me to be discharged. I told Mom before leaving there was someone I needed to see. I had to meet the nurse that sounded cruel to me. Her words hurt. I met her and let her know what she did was cruel. She had the nerve to tell me she knew I could hear her and wanted to snap me out of shock because I had been semiconscious for six months. I had to let her know it was the wrong approach. I told her it could have made me sink further into the hole of darkness. Had I not heard Mom's soothing voice, my stage level would have certainly dropped very low, but she helped me rise above the surface and into the sunlight. The day I was discharged from the hospital, I thanked all the nurses and doctors for their special care and attention. They gave me a standing ovation. There were tears and laughter. It was a very emotional day as they reminded me that I was a walking miracle. I could not wait to get home to see my dad. It didn't matter if he saw me with my head bandaged up. He would still love me anyway. Even though I felt sad that most of my beautiful brown hair was gone, I kept telling myself that Dad would love me no matter what.

When Mom and I arrived home, the rest of the family was standing at the front door with a bouquet of red and white roses from the rose garden. It made me happy to see my family once again, but most important to be alive. I couldn't compose myself anymore. I wanted to see Dad. I asked Mom where he was. She said he was in the master bedroom. Without knocking, I ran in, calling out, "Daddy! Daddy, where are you?" The bed was neatly made up. I turned and asked Mom where he was. She broke down and told me Daddy couldn't come because he had a serious fear of travelling by sea and air. However, he sent enough money to cover my medical expenses for her to travel back and forth to the hospital, and she had enough left over to make sure I had a welcome home party. I needed to know why Mom lied to me. She said she had to do or say whatever it took to help me snap out of being semiconscious.

I felt sick to my stomach. I wanted to go right back to sleep and never wake back up. However, after listening to Ma's explanation and why she had to tell me a lie, I understood her emotional pain and how she felt. As a mother, she would have gone to the ends of the earth to help her child through the grace of God get better. After all, listening to Mom tell me Dad was on his way is what helped to keep me afloat, desperately wanting to rise above the surface.

I didn't see Dr. Mohammed again until seven years later when we met by coincidence while working at the same hospital where I had surgery. Should you ever have a loved one who's unconscious or has been given a short time to live, please keep an open mind and don't give up hope. If you have never believed in a higher power before, it's time to believe, because God is real. He holds the life of your loved one in the palm of his hands. Please continue to remind your loved one how much you love them. Don't give up hope. Gently massage their hand or forehead, and talk positively to them. I know it may be difficult talking to them, but please remember they are lying in a hole of darkness and want to rise above the surface into the sunlight. They need you to help them pull through, along with God's help. There will be times you will feel frustrated and you will want to give up hope. Please don't. Continue to trust in God. Cry out and reach out to him. He may seem far away, but he's not. He's right there in the midst of it all. Try to avoid getting too emotional in front of your loved one; it can affect his or her spirit. Hopefully they will be able to hear, smell, and feel like I did. You may not know for sure, but keep talking positively to them. Avoid complaining about anything or anyone to your loved one. Know what your loved one wants most out of life. In a time of a medical crisis, it may help them to look forward to whatever it is. If it's a minor male child, about seven years old, get the nurse's permission to massage the center of his head. It may help him to feel safe and secure. They will not feel too scared. Try to spend as much time as you possibly can with them. Help the nurses sponge them, and let them hear your soothing voice. Let them know you are there to see that all goes well with them. If possible, play songs of inspiration close to their ear; it may also help. Please keep the faith and remember that God has the key to your loved one's destiny.

My physical and emotional healing had just begun. Mom had to take me back and forth to the ear, nose, and throat specialist and also to the pediatrician. Mom had her work cut out for her. Many times I wondered how much rest she ever got. She was the first person up in the morning and the last to retire to bed. My pediatrician was very pleased to know I had finally seen Dr. Mohammed but was saddened to know after all those years I had finally seen him under such crucial circumstances.

One morning during Mom's examination to my ear, she became concerned. She immediately rushed me back to the hospital. Unfortunately, it was discovered that gauze was found packed in my ear. I had to endure pain once again. As the doctor removed the gauze, I began to get dizzy all over again. When it was finally removed, my ear began to bleed. I had to be admitted until the bleeding was stabilized. Only this time I could see, move, and respond to anything and everyone. When I was finally released from the hospital, Mom would gently massage my head with olive oil. Then she would massage my temples and the back of my ear with a soft candle. Then she would gently massage the rest of my body with olive oil, reminding me that before Jesus was viciously killed on the cross, he helped heal the sick and the suffering with olive oil.

The love we give and show to children, by protecting them and ensuring their safety and well-being, we're also doing for Jesus. The blessings from God will be abundant in so many ways. On the other hand, each time you hurt a precious, innocent child, your days are numbered. It's only a matter of time before he brings you crawling, dragging you to your knees when you least expect it. To those who tug, pull, or raise a child with one hand like a ragdoll; to those who hurt or abuse children in any way; to those who are involved in human trafficking; to those who are in gangs and cause their mother's to worry and wonder where they are; to those who are murdering innocent human beings; to those who use children to make themselves money: Do you believe there isn't a higher power that knows what your game is all about? Do you think he will let you continue to get away with the very wrong things you are doing in life? You believe you can, but for how long? I would like for you to take a walk down this path with me for a moment. When you have arrived safely to your home, as you stand facing your front door with your eyes closed, find the correct key and open the door. Please for once in your life do the right thing.

Keep your bloody eyes closed and don't move until you have found the correct key to open the door that God has provided for you to step into. Remember, it's not yours. We don't own anything in life. God has only leased it to us as he leases us our lives. How does it feel to fumble for the correct key? Are you getting frustrated? Are you getting scared? Are you nervous? How does it feel to stand in darkness? Now open the darn door and get inside. As you fumble for the switch on the wall, walk over to the kitchen with your eyes still closed. Open the refrigerator and take out the drink you want. Now open the kitchen cabinet, remove a glass, and wash it thoroughly. Can you find the sink? Glide your hands along the way; it will help. Pour the drink into the glass without spilling the drink over. How does it feel to move around in darkness? It sure doesn't feel good, does it? I said to keep your darn eyes closed. Now distinguish the dime from the penny and write it down—the dime on the right and the penny on the left side. Next, place the dollar bills on the left and the five-dollar notes to your right side. Meanwhile, continue to keep your eyes shut. Walk over to the living room and find the remote control for the television. Have you found the channel you wish for yet? Now remain sitting there. How does it feel to hear the television but not be able to see it? How does it feel? Are you scared yet? Continue to keep your darn eyes shut. As you sit there, you have time to redeem yourself.

Suddenly your child is calling you. "Daddy, I'm home. I'm home, Daddy. What's wrong, Daddy? Why are your eyes closed? Can you not see me? Daddy, open your eyes." I said to keep them shut. How does it feel to be unable to see your child? Your son says, "Daddy, I need you to help me with my homework. I've got a lot of homework to do. What's wrong, Daddy? Can't you see me?" Get up from where you're sitting. Walk over to the kitchen table and help your son do his homework. Oh! I forgot—you can't, because you cannot see. Try it. Can you help him do his homework? You can't, can you? How does it feel to be unable to see your children in front of you? It's scary, isn't it? Now your child is getting scared because he can't see your eyes. He's ready to run out of the house because he cannot stand to look at you anymore because he believes you are blind. Now ask yourself if you are worthy off having the gift of life, much less the precious gift of sight along with the rest of your senses, as you continue to go on with your wicked deeds?

Slowly open your eyes and walk over to the table. Check to see if you were right in distinguishing the pennies from the dimes, along with the five-dollar notes from the one-dollar bills. You were wrong all along, weren't you? Do you think you can emotionally handle suddenly being blind? Will your spouse love you enough to remain with you, to help you through your darkest hour? Don't you dare fool yourself. You will become sloppy in everything you do until you are trained on how to do everything all over again. You will act as a child. You'll now have to humble yourself to others and depend on them to help you. It will be their time to rejoice for the wrong that you have done to them all along when you had your sight. They have waited for quite a while for something bad to happen to you, but they didn't expect this. The time has come for you to remember, "Once a man, twice a child." You will become a child all over again. Will the so-called friends you have continue to wine and dine with you? Will they continue to call you on a regular basis on the phone, as they did before you got blind? What a laugh! Don't bet your last dollar on it. How does it feel to see the light? Your beautiful children and the beauty inside your home? Have your children returned to the kitchen yet? Oh, are they still afraid to look at you, believing you are blind? Now, you don't have much time to start doing the right things in life; otherwise God will shorten it for you. You can pretend to others out there, making them believe you are all that good. In God's eyes, he can see right through every bone in your body because he has created you.

Now get to work and do the right things in life. It's time to redeem yourself and do right by God before it's too late. Make your parents proud of you. Set the innocent ones free from bondage. Treat the physically disabled and physically challenged with the compassion, respect, integrity, and dignity they deserve. They are human beings who are faced with tough challenges each and every day of their lives. You may want them to quit, get out of society. You may even want them to lie down and die or even to disappear from the planet. That is not what God says. He definitely has them here on earth for a reason and a purpose. Accept them for who they are or you disappear from God's planet. What you don't like or want for yourself, please don't wish or want for someone else. The same person you may want to disappear from the planet, you never know, that may be the same one who someday has to lend you a helping hand to cross the street. They maybe even more righteous than you are. You didn't create the world. If you have taken a life, your own life will never be the same again. Nothing you do in life will ever go right. You'll wish you were never born because their spirits will haunt you and your loved ones. Their souls will not rest in peace until you have paid for their untimely deaths. They will not rest until justice has prevailed. Who the hell do you think you are? Taking it upon yourself to commit such a heinous crime? You didn't give life! What makes you think you can take a life? And yours must be spared? Do you think you are worthy of such a gift? It's only up to God.

chapter 10

I have always reflected back on Mom's words that inspired me to get stronger and better. My hair did grow back, but it was never the same again. It didn't matter; what was important was that I was alive and healthy. I returned to the Legion of Mary. When I was eighteen, the parish priest who attended the meetings asked each member what their goals in life were. When it was my turn, I told him I wanted to enter the convent. He made an appointment for me to meet with him at the rectory. He advised me to bring my birth certificate and a letter from physician as proof I was still a virgin. I kept the appointment with great enthusiasm. When he was through reading the letter from my physician, he then looked at my birth certificate. After staring at it for several minutes, he raised his head, and with a cold expression on his face, he said I could not enter the convent because I was born illegitimately. I was stunned. To add insult to injury, he further stated that I could never enter the convent because I was born out of sin. I felt so humiliated. I just sat on the chair and wished the floor would open and swallow me up. He made me feel I was not worthy to be living in the world. It was *how* he said those words to me that made me feel sick to my stomach.

Mom instilled in us to always remember it's not what you say, but how you say it. It's not what you do, but how you do it that can have a positive or negative impact on one's life. The priest knew exactly how to make me feel like dirty mud in the world. I hung my head all the way home, asking myself so many questions. Upon my return home, I went straight to my room and cried my eyes out. My heart was breaking into so many little pieces. The way the priest said it made me feel dirty and unclean. He made it seem like it was a very clean and perfect world we were living in, and I was filth. I felt I was not worthy enough to serve God, who created me and brought me back to life. Mom knew something was wrong. She came into the room, sat on the bed next to me, and placed her arm around me. I was devastated. I could not look her in the eye. I wanted to crawl into a hole and never come back out, but I couldn't give him that satisfaction. I was not a quitter. Mom explained to me why I was born out of wedlock, reminding me that we were are all conceived out of love, and that we are a blessing and special gift from God. She reminded me to take it to the Lord in prayer. He would have the answer. He would never lead me down the wrong path.

When Mom was through talking to me, my problems seemed lighter. I didn't feel horrible; I felt reborn. Mom felt that God had given me back my life for a reason and a purpose. She let me know if I wanted to serve God, there were many other ways I could go about doing it. I could become a missionary or a member of the Red Cross Society, volunteering my time to help those who were less fortunate. Being a missionary would mean I would have to leave Mom alone to travel abroad, and I sure didn't want to leave her. Becoming a member of the Red Cross was an excellent idea.

Before I continue, I wish to reiterate to each and every one of you that it's not what you say to someone, but how you say it. It's not what you do, but how you do it that can have a positive or negative impact on someone's life—even your own child's life. You may not see or know the signs or symptoms of an individual who may be depressed or at their wit's end. What you say to that person, and more importantly, how you say it, may help save his or her life. They may have been thinking of committing suicide or committing a crime. I remember one beautiful evening, as I walked down the street, headed to the department store, I felt a cool breeze on my face. It felt so good to be alive. When I entered the store, there was a tall, handsome young man standing at the side of the counter staring straight ahead. After I paid for the item, as I was about to leave, I happened to tell the young man that whatever he may be going through in life, just feel blessed to have the gift of life and the precious gift of sight to see his loved ones and the beauty that surrounds him. As I started to walk away, he said to me how strange life is. He was waiting for his friend who was working in the back, to say "good-bye" to him. He was contemplating suicide, but my words made him consider changing his mind. Stunned, I was unable to move. After a minute, I asked him if his mom was alive. He said she was, and I advised him to think of her. Should he follow through with his plan, his mom's life would never be the same without him. She may end up suffering from medical problems. She may even go into cardiac arrest. I told him to think of her before doing something stupid. I reminded him how good it is to have the precious gift of sight to see his hands and his loved ones. I assured him the rest of his problems would fall into place. He thanked me, and I pleaded with him to hold his Bible close to his heart and cry out to God to help heal his broken spirit. I asked God to protect this young man from throwing his life away and to give him the strength to handle anything that came his way. I left the store feeling numb, praying that my words would have some positive impact on his life.

Before I officially became a member of the Red Cross, I had to be trained in CPR, First Aid, Practical Nursing, and Child Care. One day, the instructor, Mr. Paul, wanted to demonstrate how to perform CPR on a nude male manikin. The students all began to laugh hysterically, thinking it was funny. The instructor seriously warned us that it was very important to carefully watch what he was doing, for the life we may save could be very well be our own. They all calmed down and began to pay close attention. I never anticipated for one moment that several years later, I would have to apply pressure hard to my heart to help save my own life. The students and I finally completed our training successfully. It was an exciting day for us. Mom felt proud to see her youngest daughter, who two years prior wasn't given much of a chance to live after the surgery, ready and able to help others in different ways. I was now officially a member of the Red Cross. Mom was thankful that God had given me another lease on life, to help make a difference in society. The uniform was a grey dress, a white apron with a large Red Cross sign, and a nurse's cap with the Red Cross sign on the front of it. It was a joyous moment. During the ceremony, we all got to meet and greet the other members' families and express our determination to succeed.

My first assignment was working on the beach with the other experienced members and the lifeguards. On the beach, we were able to get a firsthand glimpse of how CPR was performed on drowning victims. As time went on, I enjoyed helping others. We would even bring canned food and clothing to the less fortunate ones. Every week, we the members would meet to discuss what was happening in different parts of the city. The president of the Red Cross would meet and address the members, along with the secretary, who would read the minutes. I would volunteer during the day and work at nights as a practical nurse.

During one of the meetings, the daughter of the police commissioner explained her work as a volunteer with the less fortunate. She suggested she would like to have a few members accompany her to various institutions. I was one of the chosen ones. The assignment was for two weeks. Our first stop was the blind institution for female adults. Upon arrival, we were ushered into the living quarters. One of the residents was crocheting a blanket. She looked up from her work and asked, "Who's there? I know there's someone standing there. Who are you?" She reminded me of the many times while I was semiconscious that I knew someone had come into my room. Without hesitation, Catherine replied, "How are you today?" To the delight of Ms. Jones, she recognized her voice. With a smile on her face, she beckoned us to tour the institution. Catherine introduced us all to Ms. Jones. She showed us how to distinguish the difference between a dime and a nickel, and between a five-dollar and a ten-dollar bill. She glided her fingers on the bill and the top edge. She was an expert in telling the difference. She showed us how she read in Braille. It was amazing. My heart sank seeing how content these people were, always with a smile on their beautiful faces. They didn't complain about anything, even when their loved ones turned their backs on them after learning they were completely blind. They were content with being alive. They are certainly exceptional people. We all felt blessed having our normal sight.

The next stop was the deaf and dumb institution. Spending time with the children was heartbreaking. It was a blessing to greet those special people. At sixteen, I finally had the opportunity to have my hearing corrected. Unfortunately for those children and adults at the institution, they didn't stand a chance. It was important for me to spend every spare moment I could with them. I was able to relate and understand their emotional pain and their frustration of being in a world of their own. Not being able to hear the birds whistle, listen to the beautiful music, or hear the voice of a loved one must have been very difficult for them. I was hard of hearing, and it was frustrating for me not to hear as much as I would have liked to. It sure wasn't easy. Some of their loved ones, at some point in their lives, had completely turned their backs on them, and it was obvious they felt abandoned. I hope and pray I can someday return to the beginning of my roots and spend as much time as I possibly can with those special, gifted, talented, loving people who can do so much for the world. They teach us to appreciate our numerous blessings, instead of grumbling and complaining about the simplest things in life. We never know when circumstances beyond our control can send us in different directions of having to learn to walk, talk, or do the simplest things in life that we once took for granted. The people at the institution learned to accept the fact they were special gifted people with special needs, due to no fault of their own. The smiles on their beautiful faces got to us as they tried teaching us sign language. We admired them as they communicated back and forth; it almost took our breath away.

I was fortunate to have a loving mother who took the time to nurture and care for me throughout the years when I was hard of hearing. She never gave up on me. Instead of screaming out my name, she would walk up and tap me on the shoulder and usher me to come, or she would write on a piece of paper what she needed me to do. At school, the principal and teachers were aware of my problem. They would always speak loud enough for me to hear. However, sometimes my teacher would stop and ask me if I could hear what was being said. I sometimes felt embarrassed when the kids would turn and stare at me, but I felt glad to know my teachers cared enough to check on me.

It's imperative that every parent or guardian take their children to see a pediatrician for a thorough physical examination. The pediatrician can tell if your child has an ear infection. He will give you a referral to see the ear, nose, and throat specialist. If it's not treated on time, your child can become hard of hearing or deaf. You may not know the sign or symptoms if your child has a hearing problem. Should you call your son or daughter to come to you, and they don't respond to your request, you may think your child is rude or out of control. Your child may not have heard one word you said. Even the child's eyesight is very important. Pediatricians are trained to know if there's a problem with your child's sight. Should there be a problem, the pediatrician will give you a referral to see an ophthalmologist. A simple blood test can also detect if there's any problem internally with your child. Please keep the child's appointments at all times. As a parent, it's your responsibility to see to your child's medical needs.

We also had the opportunity to visit the convalescent home for children, the same hospital where my oldest brother Lenny was admitted as a patient before he died. It was just heart wrenching to see the children there for different medical conditions. Most of them didn't have much time remaining. We were able to help inspire those children by putting a smile on their precious, beautiful faces and joy in their hearts. We brought new pajamas for them. We also found the time to comb their hair, play a few games, read, and pray with them. The children that knew they weren't going to make it told us of their fears, and we tried our best to reassure them that God and his wonderful angels were surrounding them and there was no reason to be afraid. We spent several hours with those precious children, reassuring them that everything was going to be all right. Before leaving the ward, we all prayed together. It helped to give them some peace.

I needed to know why Catherine, who came from a well-off family, wanted to volunteer her spare time to bring joy and happiness to the less unfortunate. Her answer was a simple one. She replied she wanted to do it "for the love of God" because he gave his only beloved son, Jesus Christ, who suffered and died on the cross for our sins so we could have a better life. My assignment was finally over. The other members and I had more appreciation for life, knowing we were helping other human beings who were less fortunate than we were. It helped us sleep peacefully at nights, knowing that we helped bring joy and satisfaction to others who needed it most. Mom was proud of me.

My next assignment would change my life. This chapter is very difficult for me write. I have to compose myself in order to not get emotional all over again. I have to take a breather and play my favorite CD to motivate me to continue on.

My colleague Theresa was more or less a second mother to me. She was not only older and wiser, she was also experienced in nursing. Our assignment was at the Ear, Nose, and Throat Ward, where I was admitted two years prior, and also the eye ward for female adults. We were greeted by the nurse in charge of the ward. She introduced us to the patients, using our last names. Our assignments were to comb the patients' hair, take their temperature, make their beds, sponge them, empty their bedpans, change them into their clean nightgowns, and ensure they were comfortable.

During the course of the day, I found myself drawn to this particular patient who had eye surgery and was temporarily blind. She had been there for over a week and didn't have any visitors. I took the time to cheer her up. She seemed to need my attention more than the other patients. She needed me to remain with her because she complained the nurses were mean to her. Whenever she called for a nurse, no one responded to her, except to administer her medication, sponge her, and of course to bring her meals. She further stated they were only being nice to her because we were there. After attending to the other patients, I went over to talk with her. She expressed how uncomfortable she felt being unable to see. I tried my best to reassure her she was going to be fine. As I was about to leave, she pleaded with me not to leave her. Mrs. Pieria said she felt scared because her children were away. I promised her I would be there for her and urged her not to get upset because it would only slow down her recovery. She was concerned she may not get to see her children again when they returned from vacation. I tried again to encourage her to relax and trust in God. I went on to tell her of my personal experience of not being able to see two years prior on the same floor, and how far I had come. She had to trust in God and believe he would heal her. Her life was in his hands. She thanked me for being kind to her.

As I was about to leave, she asked me my first name. I felt there was no harm in letting her know. The patient paused for a moment and then asked me my father's name. I thought of the emotional roller coaster Dad had put us through and felt it was not important to mention his name. She then asked me my mom's name. I proudly told her, and she then insisted on knowing my dad's name. She told me it was important for her to know his name. I reluctantly told her. I was about to walk away when I noticed from underneath the gauze, covered by the steel plate over her eyes, there were tears streaming down her face. I needed to know if she was okay or in pain. She reached out, felt for my hand, and said, "You are my niece."

Startled by her statement, I simply removed my hand and told her she made a mistake. I told her it was not possible. She told me I was named after my grandmother. She went on to tell me she told my dad to name me after their mother, who had passed on. I was dumbfounded. She continued to tell me where my mother was originally from and the names of my siblings. She seemed to know a lot about my family and me, but I still wasn't convinced she was my aunt. She said that my father had sent a letter to tell her of my illness and requested that she visit me at the hospital, but she couldn't. She admitted how sorry she was for sending those newspaper clippings to Dad with properties that only led to a dead end. This was a little too much for me to grasp all at once. I could not believe what I was hearing. I simply excused myself, headed for the terrace, and broke down in tears.

The emotional pain of all those years while growing up, the struggles Mom went through without Daddy at her side, and meanwhile his family enjoyed the best from his sweat and labor—and here I was assisting her while she was temporarily blind? And there she was, acting like she should get a trophy from me because she claimed I was her niece? Where was she when I needed to hear Dad's voice? Or even to hear her voice, to reassure me she would be there until Dad arrived? Where was she? She had some nerve, or was it her conscience eating away at her? I was often told of my aunt's refusal to associate with my mom, especially that one, who was the instigator.

They discriminated against Mom from the start. Back then, women were looked down upon as a "nobody" by society if they had children from different relationships. This was heartbreaking for Mom. However, she always kept her dignity. I believe this was one of the reasons why she was so strict with us; she didn't want us to find ourselves in the same situation she fell in. Her sister-in-laws didn't fail to let her know she was not in their category. In fact, she was by all means beneath them. Many nights, Mom cried herself to sleep because she didn't hear from Dad in months. His sisters didn't check on her to find out how she and the kids were doing. I was like we didn't exist. Not even one of them was there to console her when Lenny died. Where was she when Mom needed her most? They didn't even have the courtesy to attend Lenny's funeral, and here I had to clean and get the bedpan for her while she was temporarily blind. I kept telling myself this was not happening. I needed to get away from there, as far as I possibly could.

Theresa, my colleague, came to find out what was wrong. I finally caught my breath and told her what had transpired. Theresa placed her arms around me and said everything that happens in one's life happens for a reason and purpose. She went on to tell me, had I entered into the convent, I would not have had the opportunity to meet the aunt that had caused a lot of emotional pain and friction between my parents. She had even gone as far as to tell Dad over the miles across the ocean that we were not his children. I never heard any male's voice at home except my brother's. I confided in my mentor how I felt as I lay semiconscious, wanting to hear my father's voice, needing him to tell me how much he loved me and how sorry he was for not being there to see me grow up into a young lady. I further stated, each time I heard my Mom's voice, I wished to hear her say, "Here's your father." Even though he could not make it, just hearing the voice of any of his sisters, letting me know they were there, and wanting me to pull through for the sake of my dad, would have made me feel better. But he never came, and neither did any of his sisters. Theresa assured me it was God's will that brought me there to clean her. My mentor advised me to dry my tears, walk back into the ward, and act in a professional manner. Meanwhile, she would check out her story. I humbly asked her to accompany me back into the ward.

We could hear Ms. Pieria calling out my name. When we approached her bedside, she kept pleading with me not to leave her alone because she felt scared. I reassured her I was there and that I wasn't going anywhere. She continued to complain about how the nurses treated her. Meanwhile, my mentor went to check out Mrs. Pieria story. It was later confirmed that she was my aunt. I found peace within me, hearing her ask for forgiveness because she took it upon herself to tell Dad we were not his children, which caused Mom to feel humiliated. She went on to say she deliberately sent the clippings from the newspaper to her brother, so she could get rid of Mom from his life once and for all. I still could not believe what I was hearing. However, I knew how far I had come and that I could not have any animosity in my heart. I had to accept the fact it was God's will to let us meet that way.

I patiently waited until she fell asleep, and then I quietly left. When I arrived home later that evening, I told Mom of my encounter with the stranger. Mom said she did not believe it was possible. Mom said maybe, just maybe, it was another person with the same family name. The question was, how did she know I was named after my grandmother? Mom needed to see if it was actually her sister-in-law at the hospital. I said that if it was indeed her sister-in-law, please don't create a scene or embarrass me. I couldn't go into work that night.

The following day when I returned to the hospital in my Red Cross uniform, I felt the cool breeze against my cheek. I realized how good it felt to be alive as I headed toward the ward. I had to remember the oath we took. There was no turning back now. Instead, I felt sorry for my aunt. Even though she lived in a residential area in a beautiful house, I'm sure she was not happy within her soul. I met with my mentor, Theresa, whom I still greatly admire, and headed for the ward. As we entered the room, we could hear Ms. Pieria asking, "Is that you, Ellen?" I responded to her in a polite and courteous manner. After all, in spite of what may have happened in the past, she was still my flesh and blood, but most importantly, she was a human being. I continued to attend to the patients, including her. As I took her temperature, she wanted me to know how happy she felt knowing I was her niece. I didn't respond. I was still trying to grasp everything that had transpired. After sponging Ms. Pieria, I changed her into the beautiful gown Theresa and I had picked out for her. I gently massaged her ashy looking skin. When I was through combing her white, silky hair, she looked beautiful. After using the bedpan, I changed the linens and prepared her for the doctor's visit. That day was going to be the day she would know if she would ever see again. She insisted I call her by her first name, but I just couldn't. Mom arrived in time to see her before the doctor came in. As soon as Mom saw her, she said, "That's the wretch." I cautioned her not to make a scene.

Shortly thereafter, the doctor came in to check on her. After a brief conversation, he slowly began to remove the bandages. I stood aside, apprehensive to see the aunt that had instigated misery and fear. Dr. Henry cautiously continued to remove the bandages. Finally it was off. He held up his hands and asked her how many fingers he was holding. She positively answered him. He continued to check to be sure she had her vision back as she followed his instructions. Finally, he asked the nurse for a mirror for her to see her face. She was pleased at what she saw. She then saw a reflection of my face in the mirror and cried out loud. Dr. Henry wanted to know what was wrong with her. Was she in pain? Had she seen something that scared her? The nurses from the ward next door came rushing in to see what had happened. We were all concerned. The doctor was ready to send everyone out of the room when she blurted out "Oh my God! Oh my God! She's the spitting image of her father! What did I do? Oh my God! She's my niece." She kept touching my face, my eyes, and my hands. The attending physician needed to know the reason for her outburst. What was it all about? As I stood there, I felt embarrassed and wanted run away and hide, but I just couldn't. I felt stagnant.

With the nurses standing close to her bedside, Ms. Pieria emotionally rambled on about what she had done, telling her brother terrible lies about my mom. She had convinced him of the lies she had told him and her siblings, who also rejected Mom, and here the niece she refused to visit at the ward was there to help care for her. When she was through telling her story to perfect strangers, she sat up straight on the bed to get a good look at me. The nurses that had gathered around just held their hands over their mouths in disbelief. When she was finally through, the doctor said to her, "Shame on you, Ms. Pieria. Shame on you." My mom just stood there with tears running down her cheeks, shaking her head. As I led my mom away, my aunt looked over at her and humbly asked her to forgive her for what she did. Being the classy lady that Mom was, she nodded her head and said, "It's okay! I forgave you and the others a long time ago." I didn't want to see Mom upset anymore. She had already been through enough.

The nurses from the other ward just kept shaking their heads as they slowly walked away. It was a very emotional day for Mom and me. Mom later said she never thought that day would come, to hear her sister-in-law ask for forgiveness. My aunt made a promise to Mom and me that when she was released from the hospital, she would do right by getting in touch with her brother, to have him send for his wife and children. It was a somewhat joyous moment.

My mentor and I continued our assignment on the ward, caring for the other patients. She stood beside me through it all, lending a helping hand and a shoulder to cry on. Her inspiring words helped me get through what seemed to be an impossible ordeal. At the end of our assignment, we were both praised by the doctors and nurses for helping to bring sunshine and laughter to the patients. I was commended for acting in a professional manner and handling the situation with dignity.

Both Mom and I were there to escort Aunt Cara to her home in Mt. Lambert. Her children had not yet returned from their vacation to welcome her back home. We helped clean her home and made her feel comfortable. Mom stayed with her while I went grocery shopping, with my money of course, to make sure she had enough to eat and drink and prepare a delicious homecoming meal for her. She seemed humbly grateful.

We took turns taking her back and forth to the ophthalmologist to ensure all was okay with her sight. Aunt Cara had completely regained her eyesight. She told Mom it was a beautiful blessing to see that the niece that she had rejected throughout the years had blossomed into a fine young lady. She was anxious to meet Mitch and the other siblings. She thanked Mom for not rendering evil toward her. Mom's answer to her was, "Revenge belongs to God."

I continued to volunteer with the Red Cross and also had the opportunity to meet with other members from around the country.

Mitch was doing well at school, and Cindy had completed her education and was working. Aunt Cara began to visit us on a regular basis. Whenever she visited, she would hand Mom an envelope, which Mom appreciated but felt embarrassed accepting. However, Cara would say to her that it was only a small token to help compensate for all they had put her through, especially for not being there for her during Lenny's illness and throughout the emotional grief of dealing with his death.

Mom was flabbergasted when she received a registered letter and an open airline ticket from Dad. He told her of the letter he had received from his sister telling him what had happened, and said that he wanted her to come to Curacao. He left the ticket open for her to choose a date and time. He asked her to forgive him for the way he treated her and the children. Mom had not seen Dad for several years. They only communicated through letters and telegrams. Whenever Dad felt it was convenient to write and send the allowance, he did. When Mom took a much more responsible approach, Dad retaliated by taking a different approach. Sometimes when Mom received a letter from him, she would not say much; we would suspect Dad must have sent to tell her something unpleasant. One of those times, Mom sobbed throughout the night. The following day after Mom left for the garden, Mitch and I went in search of the letter. It said that should he come home unexpectedly in the middle of the night and find another man there, what he was going to do, and he didn't care of the consequences.

Mom had to make a lot of arrangements before leaving to see Dad, to ensure all was well with her children. She wanted us to continue to walk the straight and narrow path in life and to always put God first in everything we did. She reminded Mitch to focus on his education. Meanwhile, Mom's house was still the only one across the river. We continued to thank God and appreciate the many blessings we had. Mom finally left to meet Dad. She wrote to let us know of her safe arrival. She continued to write every chance she got, letting us know of the beautiful different places Dad had taken her to. She even travelled to Bon Narre. Shortly after Mom arrived in Curacao, I received an airline ticket and some money from Dad. He wanted to meet me. It was the first time I would see him since he left when I was child.

At eighteen, I was excited yet somewhat apprehensive to see him. That was what I had dreamed off for so long. While growing up as a child, the many nights after Mom tucked us into bed and turn down the lights, I silently had so many questions about Dad. "Does he ever think of us?" "Does he love us enough to surprise us at school?" "Does he sometimes wonder how we are doing?" "Did he ever love Mom?" "Did he find Mom was too quiet for him?" "Or was she not good enough for him?" I would get myself all upset by asking, "Are you a coward, Dad?" With so many questions and no answers, I would finally fall asleep. As I grew older, I realized I was only getting myself upset. It didn't make much sense. Instead, I would say a silent prayer to him. In the stillness of the night, with tears streaming down my face, I would fall asleep with an aching pain in my heart. I have said that silent prayer so many times. I finally gave up hope. Here I was a young adult, and my silent prayer was finally about to be answered, after all those years of wanting to see and get to know him. The time had finally come. As a young adult, I wondered if it was important for me to see him. After all, I was working and helping to spread a little sunshine to others who were less fortunate than I was. However, the void within my heart never went away. I guess Mom was right when she said, "Circumstances in life can take you to places you never dream of. Just hold on to God's unchanging love, and he will steer you in the right direction."

Today I'm sponsoring a little child from across the ocean. I have made a promise to her, that as long as God gives me the health and strength, I will continue to help her to have a nutritious meal, medical care, and a good education. I don't ever want her to experience the heartaches I felt waiting on a letter or the allowance from Dad from across the ocean. Every month, on the said date, she can rely on me.

I told Theresa what had transpired and my fears and doubts about going. She was thrilled for me. She wanted me to seize the opportunity to see Dad. She said to me, "You're not sure if you'll ever see him alive again." Her comments made me realize how right she was. I had dreamed of that moment throughout my life. The opportunity had finally presented itself, and I was in doubt as to whether I should go. I realized she was right. I could not pass up the opportunity. I prayed that God would keep him in good health until I saw him. I didn't want anything bad to happen to him. I wanted to have that one chance to meet and greet him, even if it was just for one time. I had to continue to be emotionally and psychologically strong.

Mindy took me shopping. She wanted to make sure I chose the right outfit, pocketbook, and shoes for the special occasion. The day finally arrived for me to travel. I looked beautiful in a pale blue dress with a white jacket, black shoes, and a pocketbook that hung on my shoulders. I looked like a flight attendant. I had already said good-bye to Mitch and Cindy before they left that morning. When I arrived at the airport, I kissed Mindy good-bye. She waited until I got clearance from customs and she saw me walk through the gates. I nervously turned and waved good-bye to her.

I finally boarded the KLM (Royal Dutch Airlines) flight to Curacao N.A. (Netherland Antilles). I prayed that nothing would go wrong. As I sat on the plane, looking through the window, my thoughts began to wander. I thought of Lenny. He didn't get a chance to see Daddy again before he died. I suddenly felt a warm feeling on my arm. I turned around to see who was touching me, but there wasn't anyone there. I sensed maybe it was my brother's spirit with me on the plane. I began to wonder how Dad would react. Will he be happy to see me? Will he find that I'm not tall or attractive enough to be his daughter? I dismissed the thoughts. The important thing was that he loved me enough to send for me.

I became startled by the heavy Dutch accent from the young man that sat next to me. He introduced himself as Rashid. The plane finally took off from the runway. Throughout the flight, I enjoyed looking at the heavenly view from the window. I wondered if my brother was looking down from heaven on me. I was certain he was in God's golden throne, watching everything that was going on. I wondered if heaven was as beautiful as the pale blue sky. Just staring at the beauty of the sky reminded me of the dream I had with Lenny and the angels. I was drawn away from my thoughts by Rashid. He wanted to know if I was on vacation. He went on to let me know he was originally from Van Krimpen Land, which is in Curacao, and that he was returning from vacation. Rashid tried his best to make me feel relaxed. He told me he was an engineer with the oil refinery. He watched my every move, as I cautiously observed him. He watched the way I placed the napkin on my lap and the way I held my knife and fork, which made me feel a bit uncomfortable. I felt like I was under a microscope. He went on to let me know that he played in a band in Curacao and that they were returning from playing a gig. Being a shy person who didn't talk much to guys, I found this young man with striking red hair to be a good conversationalist. He made me feel comfortable with his polite and courteous manners.

He was a twenty-three-year-old engineer, and I was an eighteen-year-old practical nurse. I kept a cool, calm disposition, praying that he was not a phony. I was not taking any chances. I didn't let my guard down. I kept my pocketbook around my neck, which included my important documents, along with the money I had changed in case my parents didn't come to meet me. I could take a taxi to their home.

Before we landed, Rashid wanted to know how long I was going to be on vacation and where was I going to be staying. Following my intuition, I told him. When we arrived at the airport, Rashid escorted me to customs. He seemed to be well-known by the officials. Before I could answer a question in English, he spoke in Dutch, letting the officials know who I was and other important information the officer needed. He spoke seven different languages, including Dutch. Even though I didn't speak Dutch, the language sure sounded beautiful.

When we were through collecting my luggage, Rashid walked out with me to the terminal to make sure my parents were there to meet me. As I stepped out at the end of the terminal, I felt excited. I was not skeptical or apprehensive. I was just excited to meet my father. I felt sorry for him. Besides being older than Mom, he had lost out on the precious memories of seeing his children grow up. As I stepped out into the beautiful sunlight, I immediately recognized my dad, who was over six feet tall and looked handsome standing next to Mom. As I approached my dad, he had a bewildered look on his face. The expression said it all, without asking directly, "Who on earth is that young man with my daughter?" I introduced Rashid to my parents. He was unaware it was the first time I was seeing my dad since he left us. He explained to my parents how we met. I told them he assisted me at the airport. My dad could not believe his eyes, like he was staring into the mirror. At one point in Mom's life, she had received a letter from his attorney, denying that we were his children. When Mom received the letter, she broke down. She never told us what had happened, but Mitch and I had found and read the letter. As we stood facing each other now, I wanted to say to him, "Here I am, the person you denied as your child." But I just couldn't, out of respect for Mom and the gentleman standing beside me.   The words still lingered in my ear as Mom introduced Dad to me. "This is your daughter." I was about to shake his hand when he suddenly reached out and embraced me in his arms and began to cry like a baby in the presence of my new friend. We both cried. He released me and held me at arm's length, telling me how proud he was of me, complimenting me on how I had grown into a beautiful young lady. Rashid went to retrieve his car from the parking lot. When he returned, he drove my parents and me to their home. My parents invited him to have dinner with the family, which he happily accepted. Before leaving, Rashid promised to visit us the following day.

Dad spoke Dutch, Papiamento, and English. Mom spoke a little Papiamento, French, and English. Dad tried to teach me to speak Papiamento. It was very difficult at first, but with self-discipline and determination, I began to get it together. He bought me books to teach myself to speak Dutch and Papiamento. Whenever we didn't go sightseeing, he would say to me, "This is your homework assignment."

Dad took me to see the bridge that floated while the vehicles kept on passing by. Mom took pictures of him bravely leaning on the bridge. It was breathtaking. After taking me shopping, we all went to have lunch. There were so many places to see, and there was a lot to talk about. As we sat at the table waiting for our orders, he wanted to know what my favorite hobbies were. It was a very interesting conversation on a bright, sunny day overlooking the ocean.

Every day after work, Rashid visited us. He would always bring a gift for Mom and Dad. During our many conversations, I learned that Rashid's favorite hobbies were scuba diving and playing the violin. I finally had a talk with Dad to ask why he had not visited us, and he admitted he did have a fear of travelling both by sea and air. He seemed to have an excuse for everything. I just wanted to put everything behind me and get to know my father better. My prayers had finally been answered, and that was what mattered most. I had the opportunity to meet another one of his sisters, Melinda. She resided there and had her own business but was still mooching off Dad. I was well received by her and my cousins. However, she didn't treat Mom well. She didn't want to have any part of her. Melinda just kept going on and on about how I had become a beautiful, well-mannered, young lady and how much I resembled my dad, without giving my mother any credit. She wanted Dad's permission to take me shopping with her. I couldn't continue to just stand there and listen to her flattery without acknowledging my mother for the tremendous job she did raising me and the rest of my siblings as a single parent. I had to let her know that was not the way to treat my mother. I didn't drop from the sky with my father's sperm. I was not going to go anywhere with her or Dad anymore unless they treated Mom with the utmost respect and dignity she deserved. My mother was somebody special. While growing up, she had protected me, and the least I could do was stand up and protect her as she protected me.

On that particular day, Dad finally stood up as a man and acknowledged the wrong things he did to hurt Ma throughout the years, and he promised to correct the deep, painful errors he made. For the first time in my youth, I saw a big man cry. His sister humbled herself and admitted the wrong they did toward Mom, all because they didn't like, much less respect her. She admitted that Mom was sure a "hard nut to crack." They couldn't get her out of Dad's life that easily. She went on to say that hearing what had happened with Cara, her other sister, brought her to her knees. Yet seeing my mom, she failed to acknowledge her, and that sure wasn't right. She finally embraced Mom and apologized for the horrible things they said and did to her. It was the beginning of a new chapter in Mom's life. It made her feel proud to know the child she fought so hard for was now in a position to stand up for her.

When I was thirteen years old, I decided to walk home alone for lunch instead of waiting for Mitch. One of the bad boys, who was already a man, stood idling at the corner and called out my name. Then he came up to me, held onto my hand, and began to swing it back and forth in an intimidating manner. I felt scared of Frank. Everybody in the district was afraid of him. He had spent time in prison and was known as the "district's monster." I finally found courage and told him to let go off my hand, he was hurting me. When I arrived home, I told Mom what Frank did. Mom knew I was not only quiet and naïve but also had a hearing problem, and she wasn't going to tolerate anyone disrespecting me, much less molesting me.

Everybody in the district respected Mom. They were aware she was a no-nonsense person. Mom headed down the street with her goulashes on and went to look for Frank. There he was, hanging out at the corner as usual. With all the neighbors standing there, Mom told him if he didn't want to go back to jail, he was never to speak to me or touch me again. He better let me walk the street freely, without having fear of him or anyone else. The neighbors began to clap as Mom and I slowly walked away. Mom held tightly to my hand as we headed back home. Even though he was known as bully and others were afraid of him, Mom wasn't. He never bothered me again. I always remembered how scared

I felt after the incident, but Mom made me feel safe and so brave. I was not afraid to walk the street again. The time had come for me to stand up firm and upright for her, as she did throughout my life, especially on that day and the many other times when the bullies bullied me at school. After all was said and done, Rashid was on time to have dinner with us, and it ended up to be a warm and enjoyable evening.

The following day, Dad took Mom and me to his attorney's office. I had let them know that Mitch and I read the letter he had sent to Mom and that we knew what Dad said to her about us not being his children. As a matter of fact, Mom had brought the letter with her to surprise him with it, not knowing that we had already read it and wanted to confront him when we were older, under different circumstances. At the end of the day, my father was the one who felt humiliated because I refused to go anywhere with him unless everything was corrected.

Each night when Rashid came over to visit, he taught me to translate Papiamento into English. At first it was very difficult to do, but as time went on, it gradually became less difficult for me to pronounce the words. At one point, I couldn't speak fluent English anymore. I was speaking broken English, Papiamento, and a little broken Dutch. Everything around me sounded so different. What a learning experience. Rashid politely ask my parents' permission for me to attend a function at his company. Each time he asked Dad, he said he needed time to think about it. The date of the event was approaching, and Rashid began to think my parents were not going to allow me to attend the special event. At twenty-three, he was holding a top position at the company, and I guess he wanted to impress his colleagues. Dad waited until the day before the event to give his approval, not only for me to attend the event, but also to go shopping with Rashid. He wanted me to look sophisticated at the function.

It was my first date, and the event was beautiful. Rashid treated me with the most utmost respect. He introduced me to his manager and also to some of his friends. Rashid didn't drink or smoke, and neither did I, which made our friendship more special. When we arrived home a little after midnight, my father was furious. Rashid was forbidden from ever taking me out again. That night, I found out that Dad had an investigator check his background; that's why he waited until the final day to give his approval.

Rashid asked my parents out for dinner on his day off, but Dad refused. He even invited us to visit the zoo and the museum, but my father bluntly refused. I was disappointed at first, but then I understood where he was coming from. After all, we were from two different worlds. When he said Rashid wanted to take me to those places to do to me what he can't do at home, it made me feel uncomfortable, but I realized my parents knew best. Whenever Rashid came over, I was never left alone with him. I was under the watchful eye of my parents. I had a good laugh when I overheard my father telling Mom, should he allow me to go out with Rashid, he'd have to follow us, and should he see him doing anything inappropriate, he'd definitely break his legs. They were very protective of me, especially my father. It felt good to know he was protective of me, but I knew it wasn't going to last for long.

As time went on, Rashid and I got to know more about each other. His sister was a seamstress, and his two brothers were living in Holland. Rashid majored in medicine but had to quit because he couldn't stand the sight of blood or the opening of the intestines. He came from a well-off family. He told me he grew up with a maid taking care of him and his siblings. His mother loved him very much and stood firm to ensure he got a good education. He once said to me he felt a warm and happy feeling deep in his heart for me, especially when he was close to me, but he don't know what it was. He admitted to me how happy my parents made him feel whenever he visited us. He said it was a feeling he never experience before.

During one of his days off, while he was visiting, one of my cousins, Chester, Melinda's son, came over to see us during his spring break. As I was about to introduce him to Rashid, they embraced each other and began to speak in Dutch. I stood dumbfounded, wondering what had happened. Did they know each other? My cousin excitedly stopped speaking and told me in English that they were medical students at the same university in Holland. They said they actually sat next to each other every day. Chester was a medical resident then and hadn't seen Rashid in a while. He said he heard he was an engineer at an oil company, but with their busy schedules, they lost contact with each other until then. Chester wanted to know how Rashid and I met. We both had a story to tell my cousin. After dinner, they began to translate one language into another, since they both knew seven languages. My dad joined in on the translation with what he knew. I felt honored to be in such distinguished company, but I felt silly sitting there, listening to the beautiful languages being translated. They didn't make me feel uncomfortable, and in between they would let me know what was being said. We all toasted to a beautiful evening. Before leaving, Chester and Rashid exchanged telephone numbers and promised to keep in touch. In 1968, Rashid got his blue belt in taekwondo. Two years later, he received his black belt.

Rashid asked me if I could get him a pen-pal from my country; he wanted someone I trusted. I introduced him to my friend Cassandra, whom I trusted. We both sang at the same church choir. They began communicating with each other. Rashid was interested in meeting her when he came to Trinidad. Even though we were both Roman Catholics, her parents were very strict Catholics. They were very close both to the priests and the church. To me, she was a good friend. Little did I know. Dad admitted to me later on that he was surprised to see how humble Rashid was, coming from a rich family. It didn't matter to him how rich his parents were or what fancy car he drove, the fact remained I was not allowed to go out with him again. He knew he could no longer ask for my parents' consent to take me out again, end of story. Whenever he came over, he knew my parents had a close eye on us at all times, especially Dad. Rashid was aware he had to leave at a certain time, and he sure didn't want to disrespect me or my parents. Otherwise he knew he would never see me again; Dad would have made sure of that.

I have to admit, I was afraid of guys. At the time, Rashid was the only guy I learned to trust. One night before leaving, Rashid placed his fingers around my left index finger. I asked him why he did that. He told me he wanted to see if my fingers were the same size as his. He told me he was going to Surinam for the weekend and I would see him when he returned. The time was winding down for me to return home. I thanked Rashid for being kind, courteous, and respectful to me and my parents during the months I stayed in Curacao, and I also let him know how much I enjoyed his company. It was indeed a pleasure meeting him. He was a gentleman. At the time, I'm sure there were not too many guys like him around. He was a sophisticated young man who was very cautious about everything he did. I said my good-bye to Rashid there and then because I felt he would not make it back in time from his trip to see us leave. Even though we were from different cultures, we found ourselves attracted to each other. It was difficult to say good-bye to him. He had become a close friend. After he left for Suriname, I realized I had fallen in love with him, and I was scared. He was my first love. He promised he would try to return in time to see me before leaving. We did promise to write to each other often, and he said that he would try to come over as soon as he possibly could.

Dad surprised Mom and me when he said he was returning home with us because he wanted to meet Mitch. It was time to leave the beautiful, sunny Caribbean Dutch island of Curacao. I will always treasure the beautiful memories; it was a fantastic experience. The time had come to say our good-byes to the family and friends that I met. As we sat on the plane waiting for the other passengers, I felt a bit sad and disappointed. I didn't get a chance to say good-bye to Rashid again. When I looked out the window, I saw a young man running toward the jet line. I drew the attention of my parents to the young man running on the field. I wondered how on earth he got there, and what was he thinking? I then recognized my friend Rashid. He finally came onboard the aircraft and got the consent of the flight attendant to talk to me for a minute. He then handed me a small box, beautifully wrapped, and advised me not to open it until I arrived home. He said that he just returned from Surinam, where he had bought the gift, and wanted to surprise me. He was trying to make it on time to give to me the gift before the plane took off. He then kissed me on my cheek and told me he would see me as soon as he got leave. He said good-bye to my parents. As I watched him slowly walk away, thanking the flight attendant for letting him onboard, my heart sank. I cried as I held the small box close to my heart, hoping we would see each other soon.

Dad's fear of flying was only temporary; with Mom and me at his side, he was doing fine. When we arrived home, we were greeted by Mindy, The others were fast asleep. I couldn't wait to open the beautiful gift Rashid gave me. I finally got to unwrap it. Inside was a beautiful gold ring with gold stones in the shape of a butterfly wing, with my initials inscribed on the inside. It was the exact size of my finger. I then understood why he placed his fingers around mine. He was measuring the size of my finger. I felt happy, yet sad. I had begun to miss him, wishing we could be together for a long time. I knew it was not possible, only wishful thinking. We were from two different worlds. I showed it to my parents. They commented on how beautiful it was, yet they certainly had a concerned look on their faces.

The following morning, when we all awoke, Dad saw Mitch for the first time since he left us. He was sixteen years old. He was as tall as dad and had the same thick eyebrows. They had the same features. Mitch, upon seeing Dad for the first time, outstretched his hand to shake his and said, "I'm pleased to meet you, sir." Dad suddenly grabbed him into his arms and broke down, fuming with himself, asking what prevented him for so long from seeing his son. He was inconsolable. Dad had also brought gifts for both Mindy and Cindy. He stayed a few months, getting to know us better. He got to meet my mentor, Theresa, and a few of my friends, including Cassandra, who wanted to know a lot about Rashid. What did he look like? Was he tall and handsome?

During his stay, Mom showed Dad the vegetable garden. He loved the rose garden, especially the red and white roses and gardenias. He was flabbergasted when he saw how much work Mom had put into making homemade cocoa and guava cheese. He was even more surprised walking through the corn field at the amount of corn. It was his time to help Mom pick the corn, along with bananas, pigeon peas, tomatoes, and avocadoes. He even helped Mom pick coffee, and he laughed at having to follow the sneaky fowls to find their nest and collect their pretty brown eggs. He got a firsthand look at how we lived across the river. Before leaving, Dad promised to have the house built over. He returned to Curacao, accompanied by Roberto, his nephew. He let us know that Rashid had been visiting him on a regular basis. Dad finally kept his promise.

chapter 11

Rashid and I began communicating with each other as often as we possibly could. He always let me know how much he missed me and my cooking. I anticipated hearing from him often, and he never let me down. I returned to volunteering with the Red Cross and went back to work. I brought a few beautiful souvenirs from Curacao for my mentor and also for some of the members in my unit, which they seemed to appreciate. I was taken aback when Rashid said that he wanted me to wait for him. He made me promise I would wear the ring often as a symbol that he was close to my heart. I promised I would, and I did wait for him for two years.

Shortly after Dad left, Mitch dropped out of school and gave Mom an excuse as to why he no longer wanted to attend the prestigious high school. He went on to work in a bag factory, learning to make handbags. Mom was not pleased with his decision. When Mom found out the truth in comparison to what he told her, she began to question him. Mitch finally broke down and told Mom he couldn't stand to see her struggle for him to have transportation every day, along with lunch, and also to buy other books he needed. Mitch didn't want to carry lunch to school with him anymore. He wanted to be like the other kids and buy his own lunch. He also told her he was tired of getting diarrhea from the stale meals he was having at his godmother's. Mom had arranged for him to have lunch there because she didn't live too far from the school.

The family all got emotional, wishing that Mitch would hang in there, swallow his pride, and carry the lunch Mom was preparing for him. Being the only boy, he wanted to work and earn his own allowance, and this certainly wasn't pleasing to Mom. Besides the pay being meager, he worked very long hours.

At sixteen, when he returned home from work, he would be so exhausted, he'd fall asleep in his clothes. We would have to wake him up to change into his pajamas. I became very concerned for him. He was an intelligent young man with great potential, if only he had the opportunity to complete his education. I sat down and wrote an emotional letter to the prime minister expressing our situation to him. It took a lot of courage to write him, but I had too for the sake of my brother. The prime minister had impacted the lives of so many poor people. He gave us hope to believe in ourselves. Dr. Maynard had won a scholarship and attended Oxford University in London. He experienced racial discrimination, especially when it was discovered he was hard of hearing. Unfortunately, he had to wear a hearing aid. It didn't stop him from excelling. When he completed his studies in London, he worked as a professor at Harvard University for a few years before returning to Trinidad. When he became prime minister, he gave the poor young men and women the opportunity to attend high school and college, without any discrimination, and also to get civil servant jobs. The word "illegitimate" was not to be used anymore. It could no longer be used on job application forms. He made sure there was no more discrimination in our country, especially among blacks, because he knew how much it hurt deep within. We the people loved him for who he was. It didn't matter what his opponent said about him or his hearing aid, he never let them see him sweat. He fought with honor, loyalty, and dignity for the love of the people. I explained my mother's struggles in continuing to send my brother to finish his education. I pleaded with him to help my brother. I didn't mention anything to Mom or the others about what I had done. Shortly thereafter, I received a reply from the prime minister's secretary, in response to my letter, thanking me for taking the time to write and explain the situation to him. He had sent the letter to the minister of youth affairs and said that if Mitch didn't get a response within a certain time frame, I should let him know. I was very surprised to get a response from his office. Mom and the rest of the family were dumbfounded. They could not believe that I wrote and got a quick response from the prime minister.

Mom thanked me for being courageous and brave. She said to me, "Thank you, my child. I always knew you had a gift in writing. You know how to reach out to others, to get them to hear your plea." The following week, Mitch received a letter, "Top priority from the Minister of Youth Affairs," requesting that he come in for an interview. Mitch was apprehensive and didn't know what to expect. On that particular day, Mom ensured that he was dressed in a conservative manner. She also accompanied him to the important appointment. Mom was nervous, but she tried her best to be calm. She had to be emotionally strong for her son, as she had been throughout his life. They never anticipated that they would be entering the minister's office with tight security.

Having been a country girl, living across a river, I couldn't believe that I had gotten a quick response to the letter that I wrote on behalf of my brother. I looked at myself as a loving sister who wanted to help her brother the best way I knew how. I have to admit, there were mixed feelings about what I did, discussing family business to the head chief of the country, but I felt helpless seeing Ma cry and plead with God, day and night, to open a way for Mitch to continue his education.

Mom was proud of her son and the manner in which he conducted himself at the interview. She was indeed pleased. Mitch was assigned to a Mini Youth Camp. There he would finish his education, learn a trade, and get paid. He had to leave us as soon as possible. Although we were pleased for him, we were not sure what to expect. Mitch would be away for two years and would only come home on leave. It was heartbreaking for Mom to see her only son leave home under those circumstances. Needless to say, Mitch arrived safely at the camp, along with a few other young men that were chosen. He told Mom they all had to be up at 4:00

a.m. Whenever he wrote Mom, he would let her know he was writing from the bathroom. He communicated with her every chance he got and sent her some money. He didn't have much time on his hands.

When we were much younger, we were unaware that some members at the church would pay Mom to cook their Sunday lunch. One beautiful Sunday afternoon, after lunch, I could not resist the aroma of stew chicken, macaroni pie, guava cheese, and guava jelly. I followed the scent of the aroma while the rest of the family read the Sunday newspapers. I finally found the carriers and helped myself. The stew chicken tasted so good. Mom had cooked one of the fowls from the yard, and whenever she did, it tasted so delicious. I called Mitch to help me open the can of guava cheese, and we both had a good feast. We ate so much, our stomachs were filled and we fell asleep on the floor. When we awoke, Mom was busy preparing another meal, while the gentleman and other members waited patiently for their carriers. As I hid behind the door, I overheard Mom telling the members that maybe she had given the wrong dish to someone else. I felt really bad for what we did. Mom apologized for the delay. When the meal was finally over and the members left, Mom calmly called Mitch and me into the kitchen. She said she loved us very much and she wanted us to understand that she didn't want us to ever touch or steal anything that didn't belong to us. She went on to let us know of the embarrassing position we had placed her in. At thirteen, I knew I should have known better. It was there and then Mom told us that they were paying her to prepare their Sunday meal. It made me felt guilty and ashamed for what we did. She placed our fingers over the low burner and made us repeat after her, "I will not steal or touch anything that doesn't belong to us anymore." We had to keep repeating those words after her.

When she was through, she rubbed Vaseline over our sticky fingers and sent us to kneel in the corner of our room and ask God to forgive us for what we did. Mom wanted us to respect other people's property. Mom informed us, when we grow into adults, should we see something in a store that we cannot afford to buy, or if there's something not belonging to us, we will not feel tempted to steal what's in the store or rob that person. We had to learn to be content with what we have until we can afford to buy what we want. Mom would always say, "If you see something that you want, you have to work and earn the money to buy it." She wanted us to respect authority and other people's personal property so that we would never find ourselves in trouble with the law. After that experience, we both learned our lesson. Even if we felt tempted to take the guava cheese, we would remember the punishment along with her words.

Mom told us of a true story of a young man from her country. He began to steal and rob people, and then he moved from robbery to killing. The day he was sentenced to die, he asked to speak to his mother. When she bent down to listen to what he had to say, he bit her ear and spit it out. He told her that was for her not teaching him the difference between right and wrong. Mom would say to us, she didn't want to be that mother. As we grew older, we would hear of our neighbor's children being arrested for shoplifting or armed robbery. When we see their parents holding their hands on their heads, bawling, we knew Mom took bold and drastic measures to help prevent us from being in that situation.

We also had an adopted sister, Karen. Her mother had three girls. One had run away, the other was handicapped, and Karen was a seamstress. Her mother asked Mom if she could help her. She was a quiet and shy person. She had a pleasant personality, and every one that came in contact with her just loved her. Her mother told Mom of the hardship they were facing and wanted Mom to help Karen. Her Mom complained that Karen would spend hours sewing, and when the work was completed, she wouldn't charge the customer, and they would take the outfits and walk away without even paying her a dime. She didn't speak much, and she reminded me so much of myself. We all grew very fond of her. We made her feel comfortable in her new home.

Mom sat Karen down and had a serious talk with her. She inspired her to have confidence in herself. Karen told Mom she felt ashamed to charge the customers. Mom had to explain to her that even if the customers bought the material, she had to charge them for her labor. Mom went on to explain to her that when she shows them the pattern they want, it takes time, energy, labor, and endurance to do the work. Mom let her know there was nothing to feel ashamed of; she was not robbing them. Mom helped Karen got herself established. Karen became confident in herself and made beautiful outfits that she continued putting out for her customers. Mom helped her open a savings account and encouraged her to help her mother.

As time went on, Karen began helping her mother, and they both were doing well financially. She began to have more customers than expected. Some of them even tried to take advantage of her kindness. Even though they would come for their outfits, they would claim they forgot their wallets at home. They'd ask her to give them the outfits and promise to bring the money back for her. She did so, on more than one occasion, and they never came back. She finally told Mom what had happened. On another occasion, when a customer tried it again, Mom was there to put a stop to it and stood up for her. Mom usually let the customers know they couldn't go into a store to buy their outfits and walk away without paying for it, so why do it to Karen? After Mom stood up for her, they never tried to take advantage of her again.

Everyone in the family loved Karen. She never talked too much; she was always sewing. Mom had to encourage her to take some time off for herself and go to the movies. Mitch and I loved having her around. She finally met someone, fell in love, and got married. Mom advised her not to forget her mother, and she didn't. She went on to do very well for herself.

The neighbors would come over the river and asked Mom's advice in regards to their family problems. They all loved and respected her. She always found the time to give them advice and do a good deed for someone. She never gloated over any family's downfall. She would always say to us, "Every child's pain is another mother's pain." When you have a glass house, you never throw stones. At the neighbor's request, Mom would take us with her to pray with the neighbors that were having trouble with their children, giving them words of inspiration by calling on God for his guidance. Even when the kids were released from prison, their parents would ask Mom to talk to them because they weren't listening to their own parents. Mom's inspiring words to the youths motivated them to do something positive with their lives. They would visit Mom across the river to thank her for helping to turn their lives around.

There was a young man named Paul, whose mother was a member of the church Mom attended. The mother pleaded with Mom to talk to her son, who was always running away and sleeping under people's houses. We were not pleased with Miss Agatha asking Mom to speak to her troubled son. Mom was not mothering Theresa. She was a very special person, whom we did not want to share her with every mother who had a problem with their child. Mom gave the young man a good lecture and worked with him, helping him to get himself together. He eventually did and worked on a ship, travelling around the world. Whenever the ship sailed into Trinidad, he would find the time to visit Mom, and he always brought her a gift. We always had to listen to his story of how Mom helped turned his life around.

Whenever his mother came to visit Mom, Mitch and I would have a good laugh when we overheard her telling Mom she bought some furniture and didn't have the money to give to the salesman, who kept coming over to her house to collect the money. She would have to hide under the bed as he constantly knocked on every window and door. She went on to let Mom know when she didn't have anything to cook, she would put a pot on the burner, and when it got very hot, she would throw water into it, making a loud noise, giving her nosy neighbors the impression she was cooking herself a good meal. Mom gave her a lecture about not following the "Joneses." Mom also made sure she had enough fruits and vegetables to leave with. Sometimes she would come over to our home to hide from the bill collector. Mom would have to take a firm stand and go back with her to have the furniture returned because she couldn't afford to pay for the items.

Whenever any family members came over, especially from abroad, we were allowed to meet and greet them and then would have to excuse ourselves from the living room. Mom would tell us she didn't want us hearing adult conversation, knowing more than what we should know as children. I guess this is why we try our best to be respectful of other people's privacy. Mom was like Mother Theresa. She realized she had a calling to help others who were less fortunate than her and her own children. Mom would attend services on Sundays and Thursdays, and sometimes she would be called upon to preach the sermon. She made us feel very proud to call her our mother.

chapter 12

When Dad returned to Curacao, he went back to his old ways. By then, Mom accepted the fact that Daddy would never change. Meanwhile, I slowed down volunteering with the Red Cross, but I was still a member. Shortly after I returned to the youth group in my community, I was elected secretary. There were times when I had doubts that I could type the minutes or keep up with the group's community plans. Needless to say, my loving and devoted mother assured me that I could do it every step of the way. Mom surprised me with a typewriter she bought for me in Curacao. It came with instructions for how to teach yourself to type. Mom believed in me and continued to instill confidence in her shy and naive daughter.

The president of the youth group decided to have a dance to raise money to buy typewriters and other equipment. He decided there would be a lot of people at the dance if we sold alcohol. The first time I ever went into a courtroom was to answer questions on behalf of the youth group, to apply for a liquor license. I felt scared inside the courtroom but realized the other members were counting on me to help make the dance a success. When I heard the bailiff call my name to the stand, I had to be brave for the rest of the members. In the end, we got the license and the dance was successful, but the money wasn't enough. The treasurer suggested having another dance, bingo, and other activities that would encourage the public to attend in large numbers. Everything had to be done by the book. We did make some money with contributions from businesses and some political leaders, and we finally got the equipment that we needed for the members.

The youth group had their first debate competition with another youth group who had a lot of experience. The president wanted the members of the youth group to be recognized not only in the community, but also by the political leaders that were voted into office. I was selected to represent our community by giving the closing arguments. A lot of people attended, along with their families and friends, including a few elected officials. It was supposed to be the big event of the community. I was very nervous. Needless to say, Mom was right there to reassure me that I could do it. The crowd was captivated by our group's performance and was very pleased by my final speech on the topic of teenage pregnancy. There was a standing ovation. At the end, our youth group won the competition. They received a large trophy. It was an exhilarating experience we'll cherish for the rest of our lives. Mom was very proud of me. People were complimenting Mom on the way she raised me and what a wonderful job I did. At the end of the ceremony, we returned to our loving and comfortable home, located across the river.

Even though there was no electricity, our home felt blessed with lots of love, knowing God's presence was there at all times. At the end of the evening, Mom knelt down with her children and thanked God for taking us to and from our destination safely, asking him to continue to guide, protect, and bless each and every child around the world. When we were through praying, we kissed each other good night and headed for bed. We were brought up in a loving, sheltered, yet strict home.

I successfully completed the course as a telecommunications operator and had applied to the service commission for a job. I was on the priority list and had to wait until there was an opening. Meanwhile, my friend Agnes would allow me to sit in with her whenever she worked the night shift, to get more practice. She took me under her wing and showed me the different extensions. She wanted me to learn over 350 extensions, including the operating room and the emergency room, along with the doctors who were on call for every ward, should I be sent to work at the hospital.

Mitch successfully completed his two years of training and enlisted in the army. We seldom saw him, and whenever we did, it was only for a short time. He said the training was very tough, and they sent him all over the countryside. Mom never stopped praying for his safety and well-being. At eighteen, Mitch received a gold medal for best recruit. There were two of them up for the best recruit, but Mitch got it. The other solider, Len, who was Chinese, held some animosity toward Mitch for getting best recruit. At the ceremony, their commanding officer told the large crowd it took hard work, dedication, determination, and perseverance to achieve the highest medal as best recruit. While we all cheered on, Mom was crying. She was concerned for his safety. I truly understand how she felt. Having only one son is like having one arm. Whatever you do, you certainly have to be careful you don't lose the only arm you've got.

Finally another family built a house next to us. After our house was built over, we were finally approved and got electricity. Mom and the new neighbor, Mr. Franklyn, decided that they would build a bridge. A bridge was built over the river, and we no longer had to walk over on stones, or wait for the water to go down to get across the river.

Today is Mother's Day. I feel an emptiness and profound sadness. I believe Mom is certainly in heaven enjoying her day with the rest of the mothers and continues to watch over us along with God and his archangels.

I received a letter from Rashid informing me he was coming to Trinidad on vacation. I could barely wait to see him again. I missed him very much. Shortly before his arrival, the country had a curfew due to a revolution. The day finally came when Rashid was supposed to arrive. We were limited from doing what we wanted to do. At a certain hour, we all had to be indoors. I was supposed to meet him at the airport, but no one was allowed to be out at the time he was expected to arrive. It was confirmed that he had indeed arrived at the time he was supposed to come in, but no further information was given as to which hotel he would be staying at. I was very concerned. Rashid had travelled around the world, but it was his first visit to the Caribbean of Trinidad and Tobago. At 7:00 a.m., having worked the night shift, I was exhausted. The night shift can take a toll on you. We had to ensure we took care of our health both internally and externally.

My friend Agnes and I decided to find out as much as we possibly could as to where Rashid was staying. Agnes's sister worked at the Intelligence Bureau at the police headquarters, so we decided maybe she could help. We were wrong; she couldn't have done anything, or maybe she just didn't want to that early in the morning. We left headquarters feeling gloomy. It had been two years since Rashid and I last saw each other. The day had finally arrived that we dreamed of, and the hope of seeing each other looked bleak. Agnes had already crossed St. Vincent Street, opposite the police headquarters, and was hurrying me to cross over, but I told her to give me a minute. I just stood there, staring up the St. Vincent Street sign, silently praying and wishing I could see him. All of a sudden among the crowd, I saw this striking, tall, young man calmly strolling down St. Vincent Street with a camera hung around his neck. I couldn't believe my eyes. I called out to Agnes, drawing her attention. "There he is!" I then called out to him. We were both excited, as I dangled my way across the traffic and ran up the street to greet him, calling out his name.

When Rashid saw me, he couldn't believe what was happening. We both ran into each other's arms and held on tightly to each other, not wanting to let go, but we had to. It was the first time we actually had any physical contact with each other, except a brief peck on the cheek to say good-bye. He held onto my left hand and stared down at my finger, admiring the ring he gave me in the shape of a butterfly wing. He said he wanted to see if I was wearing it. We found each other in the midst of a storm. Agnes was introduced to him. She said how unbelievable it was that out of so many other places, he was at the right place at the right time. He didn't put on much weight. He was still actually the same size. He seemed to have grown a little taller. He talked about meeting a priest onboard the KLM flight, who told him of the curfew. He was staying at the Hilton, which was quite a distance from the Intelligence Bureau's office. He told me he decided to walk down that particular street with the hope of seeing me!

Rashid took my friend and me for breakfast, and after we went shopping. He bought us a few items, including expensive perfumes. He also bought his pen pal a few gifts. He told me he wanted to see his pen pal. Agnes and Cassandra were cousins and lived in the same district. Agnes and I bid farewell and promised to see each other soon.

Rashid spent most of the day with me and my family. Having worked the night shift, I felt very tired and needed to get some sleep, but there was so much to talk about with very little time on our hands before returning to work. I called a cab to take Rashid to his hotel. We promised to see each other the following day. Upon his request, I took him to see his pen pal. As soon as I introduced him to Cassandra, she became excited. It was a bit uncomfortable for me when she began to hover over him, asking him to show her how to play the guitar, the organ, and other instruments at the same time. He had to tell her to calm herself down, he'd show her one instrument at a time. Rashid was very talented and knew how to play the different instruments at Cassandra's home. Even though I didn't have those instruments at my home, it didn't matter to him; he accepted me for who I was. He told me materialistic things didn't matter much to him.   Because of the curfew, I had to get some rest before going into work early. Cassandra promised to take Rashid back to his hotel, seeing as he didn't know his way around. We tried to spend as much time together as we possibly could, but with the curfew, it was a bit difficult. As much as we were attracted to each other, because of my strict upbringing, I could not give into his desires. I had to have self-control. One of the reasons I'll always respect and admire Rashid is that he never tried to force himself on me. He said he understood how I felt and was willing to wait until the right time. Cassandra had more time than I did. She was bold and brazen and was known for going after what she wanted. He told me he wasn't used to a woman throwing herself at him. The only advice I could give him was talk to her about the way he felt.

Cassandra's aunt, who didn't live far from my home, began spreading wild rumors, stating that her niece had taken my man from me. While I was at work, they were spending a lot of time together. Word got back to Mom. She advised me to take it slow with him. The neighbors across the street advised me to keep an eye on Cassandra, because they saw her and Rashid walking up the street, holding hands to go at the pool. It made me feel a bit jealous and uncomfortable. We seldom saw each other anymore. It all came to a halt when she showed up to my home one day and asked my mother's consent for me to go to the poolside with Rashid and her. My Mom asked her, who introduced who to whom? She went on to ask her, who did Rashid come to see? Was it her or Ellen? She didn't respond. I felt embarrassed. Mom told her, if anybody has to ask her consent for me to go to the poolside, it was Rashid. He came over and apologized for Cassandra's behavior and asked Mom if I could go with him, but Mom declined. She said he should have come and asked the question in the first place.

After the incident, I didn't see much of Rashid anymore. When I did see him, it was to say good-bye. He said he didn't expect her to behave in that manner, and he felt embarrassed by the situation in which she had placed him. He said he was leaving the following day. We promised to keep in touch with each other. I felt heartbroken. I grew up in a sheltered home and didn't have the experience some of my friends had.

As time went on, Rashid and I drifted apart. My heart continued to ache for Rashid. I missed him terribly. However, I kept myself busy and never spoke to anyone about how heartbroken I felt. Throughout the years, I suppressed my feelings deep down inside. Back then, waiting for a loved one overseas was very emotional. There were no calling cards, and long-distance calls were very expensive. Added to that, there were no computers available to the public. Today it's different. You don't have to wait on the postal delivery, hoping and praying the postal workers don't ever go on strike. Whenever they did, you silently prayed the strike would end as soon possible. Meanwhile, you kept on working and occupied yourself doing positive things to help the time pass by quickly. You hoped and prayed your letter didn't get stuck in the mail as you awaited a reply from your loved one.

After Rashid left, I found out that Cassandra went to Curacao. Shortly after her return, her cousin said she had gotten involved with her sister's fiancé, which caused chaos in the family. Unfortunately, the sister ended up in a mental hospital. Later, she got better and put the pieces of her life back together. She returned to living a normal life and forgave her sister. With a lot of love, prayers, time, and patience, they all became a happy family again. Before getting married, she had to get the young man's parents' consent. She had gotten pregnant, and as strict Roman Catholics, her parents would not allow her to have a child out of wedlock. Her parents finally forgave her for the emotional pain she inflicted on them and her sister. She had three beautiful children. Shortly thereafter, her husband, Angoon, resented her and went back to her sister. Needless to say, with her beauty, charm, and charisma, she knew how to seduce her man back into her arms. She broke a few hearts along the way to get what she wanted. It took some time for us to speak to each other again, but I understood where she was coming from. She grew up in a strict Catholic home and was not allowed to go on dates. She didn't have much freedom. Meeting Rashid gave her the freedom she needed to express herself and to get away. She later told Agnes her biological clock was ticking away and she didn't want to end up an old maid.

The patient I had been privately caring for had died, and jobs had become scarce. I got a job as a bartender in a pub not far from home, as I patiently waited to be called in as a telecommunications operator. Opposite the pub was the inn, owned by the same owner. Each day I arrived at work, I would look at the inn and silently pray that I would get transferred to work there instead. At the pub, I had to learn to mix drinks, take orders, and use the cash register. Fridays would be very crowded. The young people would come in from near or far to shoot pool or sit and chat. Sometimes the manager would come over to see how things were going. At the end of the evening, I would have to turn in all receipts and cash out, ensuring all was correct. Sometimes I had to handle a lot of money. I had to ensure that every nickel and dime was accounted for. I couldn't afford to make a mistake. After a while, my male coworker began to give me a tough time. In his eyes, I did everything wrong. There were so many times I just wanted to quit, but Mom would advise me to hold on and keep praying. She would remind me half a loaf was better than nothing.

The day came when I went into work and learned Michael was on sick leave. When he returned, he said he needed to talk to me. He apologized for the way he had been treating me. He went on to say he felt attracted to me and didn't know how to express himself; it was easier for him to constantly nag me. He said he was sorry he didn't take my advice about smoking pot. He was admitted to the mental ward, and he hoped I would forgive him and continue to talk to him. Back then, if someone ended up in the psychiatric or mental ward, it left a stigma on the person. No one wanted to associate with that person again. He showed me respect, and we remained mutual friends.

One day, I received a call from the manager. He wanted me to start working in the dining room over at the inn right away. Michael was left to tend to the pub until he got another coworker. There was also the hotel, which was located on both sides. There would be a lot of tourists who came on vacation. Weekends would be very busy. During the week, I worked the night shift from 4 p.m. until 12:00 a.m. On weekends, I worked until 1:00 or 2:00 a.m. The manager explained that the salary was not much, but I could earn much more in tips as long as I served the customers well. I started setting the tables, making sure the water glasses were in their places. I was shown how to make a flower design with the napkin before placing it into the glass. Not long after I was through setting all the tables, the customers who had reservations began arriving early. At first I felt a bit apprehensive. Brenda, the maître de, said to relax and that she would be there every step of the way. During the night, she gave me most of the best tables, customers she knew who tipped well. I did my best to ensure the customers were well served. Brenda suggested that we pool together. She was a very nice person with a pleasant personality. Gradually we became good friends. She would confide in me her personal problems.

Mom, my nephew (my brother's child), and I were living at home. My sisters had moved out and had a family of their own. I hated working on Sunday nights. When the shift was over, most of the waitresses would be headed in one direction, and I was the only one would be heading in the opposite direction. It was very lonely waiting for transportation. There was seldom anyone on the streets on a Sunday night, especially after 8:00.

One Sunday night after work, I stood alone waiting for a cab. Finally a cab arrived. I knew the driver but didn't know all the passengers. When I arrived at my destination, as I got out, a young man got out too. He began to follow me. When I stopped walking, so did he. Scared out of my wits, I stood frozen, hoping the driver would see what was happening. I refused to walk down the gap, heading toward my home. Even though the light for the yard was on and very bright, it couldn't have shown straight up the gap leading to the road. I usually walked with a flashlight, but I still didn't want to take any chances. The driver saw what was happening in his rearview mirror. Instead of continuing on his journey to drop off the other passengers, he reversed in our direction and began to blast his horn loudly. The noise had the neighbors turning on their lights to see what was happening. Maybe the young man was more scared than I was; he took off running. It was a very scary experience for me. The driver wanted to know if I was all right, but I was pretty shaken up. I thanked him for being alert and asked him if I could make arrangements for him to pick me up after work every night. He said yes and we agreed on a price. He continued to flash his lights and waited until I was safely across the river and at the front door. Rover must have smelled me coming home. She began to bark and ran to greet me. I couldn't have been happier to see her as I gave her a tight hug. When I arrived home, instead of being in their beds, my mom was standing at the front door, and my two-year-old nephew was sleeping on the couch. Mom said he got of his bed and joined her on the couch to wait for me. On that particular night, God and his angels were certainly looking out for my safety.

Shortly thereafter, I went to Grenada to get to know the rest of my family on my mother's side. I had the opportunity to visit my beautiful grandmother. She was very excited to see me and get to know me better. She avoided the sensitive topic of why she left Mom and her siblings, and I certainly didn't want to push it. I was very impressed with her vegetable garden. She showed me how she grew nutmeg, cloves, and fruits, including sugar apple. Grandma went on let me know the cinnamon sticks are boiled and drunk unsweetened to control diabetes and other health issues. She showed me how nutmeg is placed inside of the mouth, on the same side that has been swollen or twisted due to a stroke. She advised me, should l ever get a stroke, regardless of how minor the problem is, I should continue to suck on the nutmeg until my speech has returned to normal. Grandma also took me to the fruit and vegetable market and introduced me to all her friends, letting them know that she was proud of her granddaughter.

I admired Grandma and how she kept her home sparkling clean, along with her china. As soon as she was through using the chine, she dried it and neatly put it away. After spending some time with her, I understood her fears. I tried my best to reassure her she was still a special child of God and to remember at the end of day, should any one of us find ourselves flat on our back, unable to move, the color of our skin, our job title, and our financial status don't matter. It's up to a higher power to reach out and touch us with his miraculous hand, to heal and bring us back to life. He's the only one to move the stubborn mountains that stand in our way of a full recovery. She was a loving and wise person, who was denied the right to be with children all because of the color of her beautiful skin.

I was impressed at how humble my cousin Alicia was with everyone. Even though she was the wife of the police commissioner, she never looked down on anyone. She was loved by everybody. She always found the time to help her neighbors and those who needed her help in caring for their children. She also boarded young men and women who were from the countryside of Sauteurs and Gouyave in Grenada, civil servants that included police, prison officers, and teachers who were working in the city. Every day she had a buffet for them at her beautiful home in St. Georges.

I also had the privilege of meeting another uncle. Unfortunately, I learned that my aunt was being abused. I wanted to leave, but she insisted I stay. I have to admit, I was concerned she would be mean to me, but I was wrong. She was very kind and gracious to me during my stay there with her family. I tried my best to encourage my uncle to get the professional help he needed with his alcohol problem. It worked for a while, but he went back to his old ways. When he didn't drink, he was at his best behavior. He was very nice person except when he drank. Before leaving, I took the ring that Rashid had given to me and offered it to my aunt as a token of my love and appreciation. I sincerely hope it was able to help heal some emotional wounds. She doesn't know the story behind the ring. She has since moved to Canada and is doing well. Unfortunately, later on, my uncle died.

chapter 13

My training at the telephone company was tough. The instructor was strict and wanted us to do our best wherever we were sent to work. She advised us to study over the weekend because we had a final test coming up. Besides working on the board, we had to know the correct way to answer the phones. As she would tell us, you never know who's at the other end of the line. On that particular day, we were all nervous. She wanted us to have a trial exam before giving us the final. When she was finally through grading our work, she told us we all did a great job; we passed with flying colors, and it was the final exam. We couldn't believe it. It was finally over.

I was finally called in to work at the General Hospital as a relief telecommunications operator, so I would not be getting a salary anytime soon. I explained to Mr. Manson, the manager at the inn, that I was called in to work at the hospital and would not be able to work full-time anymore. He said he found me to be an honest and hard worker and would like me to stay on part-time. He said depending on the shift I had to work, he would do his best to accommodate me. I appreciated that very much.

At the hospital, I had to know all the extensions for the different wards, including the ward where I was admitted at the age of sixteen. I also had to know who the doctors were on call for every ward. As an operator working for the government, it's only four hours, and we feel blessed for that. From the time we started work, we were constantly talking. The time limit helped us to protect our vocal cords and prevented us from getting serious diseases in our throat. Sometimes I would get hoarse, until I got used to it. I gargled apple cider vinegar diluted in water to kill any bacteria, and then had a cup of tea with lemon and honey to protect my vocal cords. Working the night shifts was tough. There would be two operators, and sometimes an operator would call in sick and I would have to work alone. The nights were long and I had to be alert at all times, because a life depended on how fast I could get the doctor on call. Sometimes, when it was slow, the doctors didn't always stay at their quarters; they might have gone out to dinner. It was imperative that they let the operators know where they could be reached at all times in case of an emergency.

Whenever I worked the night shift at the inn, I got home after 2:00 a.m. Then I had to be at work at the hospital by 7:00 a.m. When I was through at the hospital, I would return home, get some rest, and then go back to work at the inn. When I worked the night shift, I couldn't sleep much during the day. However, the job at the inn, mostly the tips, helped support me until I got paid from the hospital, which would sometimes take over three months. With the weather hot most times, having a cold shower kept me cool and helped me make it through my different shifts. I hardly had any appetite to have a good meal. Nevertheless, I always had a glass of milk with sanatogen powder and multivitamins to help strengthen my immune system. It helped to give me the energy and stamina I needed to remain focused.

One evening, while working at the hospital, there was a call from the operating room from Dr. Mohammed, requesting a call to India. I could not believe my ears. I distinctly remembered his voice and his accent. I reminded him who I was and the many disappointments and humiliations Mom went through whenever she took me to see him, until he finally did the surgery. His reply was, "Oh yes! I remember you. I'll be right down."

When he arrived at the operator's booth, we shook hands and he warmly embraced me. He said that even though he knew it was major surgery and that it would take some time for me to recover, he knew I would make it. He humbly apologized for the humiliations his nurse had put my Mom through to see him. At the courtesy desk, I put through the call for him to India. When he was through speaking to his party at the other end, he gave me a note to take to Mom. Most of the doctors and medical residents were from different parts of the world. Whenever they needed to make a long-distance call, they could take the call from anywhere they wished. We had to log it when they were through talking. It was the operator's responsibility to call back the local telephone operator to find out how many minutes they spoke for and then charge the doctors. Otherwise, we would end up paying for the call from our pockets, and I definitely couldn't afford it. Whenever the local operators gave the fee and the amount of minutes they spoke for, they couldn't believe it. Back then, it was very expensive to make long-distance calls. They would be so happy to speak to their loved ones, they would get carried away, without checking the minutes they were on the phone.

When I arrived home later that evening, I gave Mom the note from Dr. Mohamed and told her of my encounter with him. She couldn't believe it. He invited Mom to meet with him to have lunch, and he apologized to her for what she had endured throughout the nine years we desperately traveled miles to see him. There were tears of forgiveness. As Mom used to say, "God may not come when we need him, but he's certainly there on time." It had been a very long journey for Mom and me. This is why it's so important that I sincerely do this to honor her for the many trials and tribulations she went through for me to have a healthier life. I tried my best to do this before she passed away, but sadly it wasn't meant to be. I'm sure her spirit above is helping to guide me, especially when it becomes too emotional for me to continue.

Even though Dad took his time, he finally kept his promise and paid the contractor to build a bigger house for her to live in. Mitch bought Mom a big refrigerator. My other two sisters and Mitch helped to wire the house. The first time Mitch had Mom turned on the lights in every room, it looked heavenly. We all got emotional, thanking God for his wonderful blessings. We no longer had to use the lamps. However, Mom always kept them close by, just in case the electricity went off. We had come a long way, and we were thankful for the many blessings we had.

For the Christmas holidays, I finally got paid from the hospital and bought Mom an electric stove. Mitch bought her a large ham, and Mom baked it, along with black cake in the oven, instead of the makeshift oven outside in the yard.

As time went on, I got transferred to the prisons. I dreaded working there. As soon as I entered the prison, the slamming of the loud gates behind me would send shivers down my spine. I couldn't wait for my assignment to be over. The only contact I had with prisoners was the orderly ones on good behavior that cleaned the yard and the operator's booth. A prison guard was always present with me in the booth. One particular day, the prison guard had stepped out for a minute when the van transferring other prisoners to the island, which is where the really bad prisoners are sent, stopped at the gate. A prisoner stuck his head into the net and pleaded with me to call and let his mother know where he was being transferred to because he was unaware they were going to transfer him. Scared out of my wits, as I was about to ask him his mother's name, the guard returned and said, "Sure, she'll get in touch with your mama."

One day, I was called into the superintendent's office. As I was about to climb the stairs, I heard loud whistling noises. When I looked down, there were several prisoners who were on their hour break, staring up at my skirt from the hole in the yard. I raced nervously up the stairs as fast as I could to the office. I just couldn't wait to complete my assignment. Every day, I would have to use a code to call the other prisons to check on how many prisoners were onboard, in sick bay, or attempted to escape and then log it in before assigning over to another operator.

There was the prisoner, Frank, who was serving time for raping his stepdaughter. He was an orderly prisoner who had gained the officer's trust. The day came when he was released from jail. Before leaving, he came into the office to say good-bye. We all wished him well in society. About a month later, I had completed taking the nurse's exam and was heading outside. It began to rain heavily, with the heavy wind, my umbrella broke. Another student, Michelle, who sat the exam with me, offered to share her umbrella. As we continued to walk, we discussed how tough the exam was. She told me she was from Point Fortin and didn't know her way around Port of Spain. She went on to let me know she was engaged to a contractor and was planning to get married soon. She asked me if I could accompany her to the hospital gate because she was expected to meet her fiancé there. I told her I would because I had to take a cab from there to get home. When we arrived at the gate and she introduced me to her fiancé. It was Frank, the prisoner that had recently been released. As I stood there facing him, the expression on his face said it all. He then stretched out his hand to me, and I did the same. I gathered from the conversation he had with her, he didn't tell her of his past conviction. I wished them both the best of luck and continued on my way. When I arrived home, I told Mom about the coincidence and asked if God was trying to tell me something with all these coincidences. She said God wanted me to know how powerful he is.

A few days later, when I returned to work, Frank came and thanked me for not saying anything to his fiancée. I told him he was starting off on the wrong foot. He should be honest with her, and their relationship should be based on trust. He had already paid his debt to society, even though his victim would be scarred for the rest of her life. If his fiancée really loved him, she'd forgive him and try to move on with their life together; otherwise, sooner or later, eventually the truth would come out. Shortly thereafter, his fiancée came to see me at work and thanked me for the advice I gave to Frank and also for not embarrassing her with what I knew. I was baffled by the encounter I had with the ex-convict. I often wonder why I was there in a position to see, hear, or know certain things. My assignment was winding down, and I couldn't wait to leave.

Monday morning when I arrived at work, the prison guard on duty told me that shortly after I left on Friday, I had a visitor. He said it was a prison officer from the island prison that came on his day off to see the person behind the beautiful voice. Before leaving that Monday, a handsome young officer who had returned from vacation came in the booth to say hello. He said he was interested in me and wanted to take me out for dinner. I couldn't help admiring his pretty grey eyes. I told him they reminded me of my friend's baby's eyes—although I didn't mention her name, Agnes. He then asked me where I live. I told him, and he smiled and said he recently had a baby in the same district. Both the mother and child lived there. I advised him not to neglect the child that God entrusted to him. That was the end of the conversation. I was then assigned to National Security. My friend Agnes ended up working at the same hospital. She told me her daughter's father was working at the prison and was denying that the child was his. I asked her his name, and when she told me, I realized it was the same gentleman I met. I told her about meeting him and reminded her how much his features resembled the child's. She couldn't believe it. Not long after our conversation, she let me know he came and visited the child and bought several items for the baby. He told her of my encounter with him and was brazen enough to let her know he tried flirting with me. Today, that child is a teacher and the wife of a pastor. Her mom and I still communicate. We have been there for each other throughout the good and bad times. My goodness, how time flies.

When I arrived at my part-time job at the inn, the manager called me into his office and asked if I could get a few waitresses to work at the inn. He said he had confidence in me to get the best waitresses whom I trusted. I was reluctant to do so, and he realized I was not pleased by his request. I told myself, should anything go wrong with them on the job, I may have to take the responsibility. He said he trusted my judgment and was counting on me. I believed he wanted to save time and money by not putting an ad in the newspaper. At the same time, I realized he could have asked somebody else, but he chose me. I took it as a compliment. I confided in Mom, who praised me for him having that much confidence in me. At the time, I could not think of anyone for him to hire. Mom finally helped me consider a few of my trusted friends. Before taking them in to see the manager, I was apprehensive. I advised them to dress conservatively and to conduct themselves in a professional manner at all times. They were hired and earned the respect and admiration from the management and staff.

One night, as I leaned against the terrace enjoying the cool breeze, waiting for the guests to finish their dinner, Michael, the head waiter, told me he was interested in me and wanted us to have an intimate relationship. It had always been my policy not to have an intimate relationship with a coworker because I believe at some point, they lose respect for you on the job—and besides, he was my friend's boyfriend. In a calm tone, I told him I couldn't because he was already in a relationship with the maître de, who was my friend, and it would certainly be disrespectful to her. He decided that instead of me continuing to serve the guests, I had to clean the tables. I felt deeply hurt.

The salary was not much, and I had not seen a check from the hospital in a while. I depended on the tips. I confided in Mom, and she told me I made the right decision and to stand my ground. She advised me to continue to pray that I would get a permanent position. It was becoming tiring, especially travelling the long distance, sometimes taking over an hour to get to and from work and back to the inn. From National Security, I was transferred to a few other ministries, including the board of education, and then back to Port of Spain. Sometimes, when I was off from the inn, the manager at the inn would call me at the hospital to come in to work because he was short-staffed. He would promise to pay me double time, even though I would explain to him I couldn't leave unless I was relieved. He understood but would insist I still come in. I would promise him I would do my best.

As time went on, Michael was determined to make my life unbearable. He would have me clean the dining room tables all alone. When I was through clearing all the tables, he would have me back and forth, up and down the stairs to the rooftop tables. Then I would have to go back into the dining room and serve drinks to the customers. Sometimes I wanted to quit, but Mom advised me to hang in there and keep on praying. Hold on to God's unchanging love and don't give up. Sometimes I would go into the ladies' room and break down in tears. It was beginning to get to me, but I refused to be subjected to his demands. He was the type of person no one said no to, but I couldn't say yes just because he wanted his way. This was my life, and I had a choice to live it how I felt was right. He wanted to take my freedom away from me, and I couldn't let him. He cared about nobody but himself. I don't think he even respected himself.

One night, as I was about to have dinner, Michael told me I was no longer allowed to have dinner at 7:00 p.m. or sit at the poolside to eat. Instead, I would have to eat in the kitchen or at the back of the kitchen. He also said I would be having diner between 11:00 p.m. and 12:00 p.m. or at the end of my shift, depending on how crowded it was. Sometimes, I just couldn't eat. I would take my dinner home with me instead. By the time I arrived home, I still couldn't eat. I didn't have an appetite anymore. I took it all in stride, praying that there would be a better tomorrow. On that particular Friday night, it was very busy in the dining room, and with enough workers on the shift, I decided to have dinner at midnight, as I was told. As I was about to have dinner, I received a call from the manager saying he wanted to see me in his office. He sounded intoxicated. As I entered his office, I could smell the heavy scent of alcohol on his breath. He told me the head waiter told him I was no longer doing my job in an efficient manner, and should he get another complaint, he would fire me on the spot. He wanted me to go back into the dining room after dinner and work with efficiency. I felt heartbroken; it was too much for me. He never asked me if it was true or false or what had happened. I could not believe my ears. The same person that claimed he trusted me and that I was a hard worker never asked me for an explanation. His mind was already made up, and I never said anything to him or to Michael's girlfriend; instead, I kept it all inside.

I could not take any problems with me to the job at the hospital. I had to remain focused at all times. One slip up and the operator could get into trouble. I continued to pray for a miracle. I didn't know how much more I could take. My sisters had their busy family life. Whenever they came to see us, I would be going into work. I didn't know what it was like to have a meal at home with Mom anymore, especially on a Sunday. My lunch was merely a snack. I seldom saw my brother. If he wasn't in a classroom, he was transferred to some other part of the country. Whenever I did see him, it was only for a short time. However, it would be a joyous moment to see him spend time with his son. The love between a father and a son is unbelievable. He was able to give Markus the love he didn't get from Dad. It was heart wrenching to hear my nephew cry whenever his father had to return to the base. Most times, he would return and take him for a drive. When he returned with him, he would have to explain to him that he had to be at work at a certain hour and the drive to get there was quite a distance.

Meanwhile, I was helping Mom raise my nephew. I would find the time to take him to lunch or to the park, teaching him to play football or taking him with me to play lawn tennis. I didn't have much of a personal life. If I wasn't working, I was home doing the laundry or weeding the grass, which was sometimes a tough task to do. Depending on my shift, after I dropped Markus off at school, I would return home and continue to root up the weeds before I went into work. Mom was my solid rock. I could talk to her about anything, and she always had a positive, constructive answer for me. Even as an adult, I never felt I was too grown to talk to her. During the rough times, her loving arms comforted me, and I always felt very safe being with her.

I still found time to be a member of the Red Cross. Sometimes we were invited to attend different parades, including celebrating the anniversary of independence. There would be a drill master from the army to teach us the correct way to stand, keeping our posture straight at all times, especially during the parade. The drilling was tough, but we enjoyed it. One day, I arrived home from the Independence Parade and my nephew was waiting for me at the front door. As soon as he saw me, he excitedly said, "Auntie, I saw you marching on TV! You were marching good!" He felt very proud seeing me march at the parade with my Red Cross uniform on. It was exciting seeing Mitch march with the army. We would have good laugh meeting up at the parade. When his unit was through marching at the parade, he would then head for the barracks and be transferred to another part of the country. During the carnival season, we were assigned to different posts. Sometimes there would be three or four of us, and we all had to remain together. It's a time when a lot could go wrong, especially when the bands are going straight into the stands for the competition.

One year, I took time off from attending to injured people and ushered during the carnival season at the carnival stands to make an extra dollar. It was fun ushering the people to their appropriate seats and making sure they were quite comfortable. I got a chance to see the various artists perform and the band competitions. Actually, it was the first time I got to see carnival. I was never keen to see it before that. It was quite a distance from where we lived. The band leaders spent many days and nights working on different costumes. Tourists would come in from London, Holland, and other parts of the world for the special occasion and take part in playing in a band of their choice. When it was all over, the tourists would return to their different hotels, including the inn, and we—the waitresses—were constantly on our feet, bringing them room service. Sometimes we wished they would make up their minds about the exact order they wanted instead of having the waitresses go back and forth with a different order. Sometimes, if the kitchen was closed, the manager would ask me to make a grilled sandwich for the guests. Besides the problem I was experiencing at the inn, I got the opportunity to make different drinks and learned the difference between a medium, rare, and well-done steak. Sometimes, when the kitchen was closed and a guest came in late for dinner, the manager would send one of us in the kitchen to prepare him a steak or even a shrimp cocktail. If the desk clerk was off, the manager would call me in from the dining room to answer the switchboard and check in or check out the guests. The manager was aware of my training with the Red Cross.

One night, while working in the dining room, he called for me to attend to a guest. She had cut her finger on a broken mirror. After attending to her, I told him she needed stitches and a tetanus shot. The guest claimed she never had a tetanus injection before. Instead of waiting for an ambulance, he had his personal driver take her straight to the hospital, waited for her to get taken care of, and took her back to her suite. She received a tetanus shot and several stitches. Before she checked out, he gave her a discount on her bill, which was just great.

Another night, the manager called me in from the dining room to attend to the front desk. Before leaving for an important function, he advised me of the guests and the rooms they were staying in. They had to check out at a certain hour. He wanted me to be on the lookout for any of the guests who might try to skip out on paying their bill. As responsible adults, they should be honest enough to pay the bloody bill. I felt I shouldn't have to look out for them, because I was not a watchdog. A section of the hotel was located behind the lobby; it was plain out of sight. However, once there were guests staying at that location, you always had to be more alert. One night while I was attending to the switchboard, a young man came in and went upstairs. Several minutes later, he came back downstairs with the guest's suitcases, placed them in his car trunk, and went into the driver's seat and waited. Several minutes later, the guest came downstairs and handed in his keys but didn't pay his bill. He was heading toward the car. I had to draw the security guard's attention to have him return to pay his bill. When he came in, he said he was only going out for a spin and that he would be right back. I had to remind him of his checkout time. With security standing close by, he paid his bill and politely left. I understood it had happened before, and the clerk had to pay the bill. I wasn't in a position to pay for someone else's bill. It just wasn't right at all. The manager heard about it from the security guard and complimented me on being alert. Right! I was the worker of convenience, doing other jobs for one salary, and yet having a difficult time with his trustworthy worker who in his eyes did no wrong.

I didn't know how much more I could continue to take. I needed the job. At the time, other jobs were hard to get. Even the bartender began to give me a difficult time because he asked me out and I said no. I couldn't believe what was happening to me. I seemed to be an easy target for those hungry wolfs. He even gave me a difficult time when I tried to get the drinks to take to the customers in an orderly manner. Finally one night, one of the guests saw me standing at the bar, repeating the drinks I wanted while the bartender continued to attend to the other waitresses. The guest came over to the bar and told him what he witnessed. He said if he didn't give me the drinks immediately, he would report him to the general manager. That straightened him out. I got the drinks right after the guest spoke to him.

The harassment continued by both the bartender and the head waiter. I finally turned to my friend who was a detective and explained what I had been experiencing. He promised he would try to help me. He surprised me when he came in one Friday night with his colleague and sat at the bar. They observed my every movement and what was taking place. They got a firsthand look at how I was treated by the workers and why I just wanted to crawl into a hole. It's one thing to be humiliated in front of your coworkers, but it's another thing to be humiliated in front of strangers. You feel dehumanized. After work, they met with each worker and told them what they saw during the time they were there. They gave them a stern warning to show me respect. I thanked my friend David and his colleague for taking the time to help me. Time and again, my friend would stop by unexpected to see how things were going. Sometimes the workers would continue to give me a tough time, but upon seeing my friend and his colleague, they would ease up on me. Today, David and I continue to remain close friends. In spite of our busy schedules, we still find the time to communicate with each other. He'll always hold a special place in my heart. I'll always appreciate what he did for me.

I became concerned for my health. I began to get hoarse on a regular basis. I had to do a lot of talking at the hospital and then at the inn, having to speak up loudly with the music playing in the background and the guests chatting away. A specialist at the hospital said my vocal cords were strained. He said I should take some time off to rest my vocal cords. I had to follow his instructions so that I didn't sound like I had swallowed a frog. Shortly thereafter, while I was working the evening shift at the hospital, I received a call from the head waiter at the inn. He told me he needed my help. I wanted to disconnect him for what he had put me through. And now he needed my help? Back then, there were no laws to protect men and women from sexual harassment on the job.

Instead of disconnecting the call, I listened patiently to hear what he had to say. After all, I still had to go into work there, and I certainly didn't need any more drama. He finally broke down and asked me if I could help him find him a good doctor. According to the way he had treated me, I was just a quiet, naive person. He looked down on me like I was a nobody. So why would he need my help? He finally confided in me that his girlfriend had an abortion and was continuing to bleed profusely, and he was scared. I advised him to take her to the nearest hospital. He said he didn't think she was going to get the help she needed. She was a human being, and I couldn't take revenge on her for how he had been treating me—even though she would just stand there while Michael tormented me in the presence of the guests, without saying a word to him. I immediately turned to a doctor I knew and trusted. He was a skilled and gifted young doctor from South Africa. He told Michael what he had to do before bringing her into the hospital. I later learned, had Brenda waited a few more minutes, she would have hemorrhaged to death. She had lost a lot of blood. He waited until it was bad enough to seek professional help. She had to have emergency surgery to correct the damage that was done to her. Thank heaven, everything turned out just fine. She made a full recovery and went back out to work. I felt peace within my soul because I was in a position to help her get the best care she needed.

I told Mom what happened, and Mom reminded me to continue to trust in the Lord, for he said, "Sit down at my right side," until he brings your enemy to his footstool. Mom's words always had a profound effect on my life. Mom always reminded me that I was a special child of God. She would then say to me, "Many are called, but few are chosen, and you are one of God's chosen ones." I can't help getting emotional thinking about the way I was treated on the job. Maybe they assumed I was making a lot of money and wanted much more. Little did they know, most times I didn't see a dime for months. When I did receive my pay, I had my share of responsibility in helping to pay the bills. I have to admit, sometimes, I felt frustrated. I seemed to be working for free, but with Mom's help, I continued to hold on and didn't quit. Meanwhile, I was still off from the inn.

While working at the hospital, I was surprised when I received a call from the manager at the inn apologizing for what he had said to me in regards to the performance of my job. He went on to tell me, he learned there was a misunderstanding. I couldn't believe what I was hearing. He was not the type of person to apologize to his employees. He then asked me if I could come in to assist at a cocktail party; he would pay me double time. I felt exhausted, but I needed the money, and besides, I didn't want to disappoint him. That night, I arrived at the inn at 7:30 p.m.

The receptionist at the desk informed me that the manager needed to see me when I arrived. I did mention to him, seeing that I was off from the inn, I didn't have my uniform with me. He assured me that one would be provided for me when I arrived at work. When I entered his office, he thanked me for coming in even though I was tired. He once again apologized for what he previously said to me and then handed me a package with a new uniform to change into. As soon as I was through changing, I headed straight to the rooftop. Michael greeted me at the top of the stairs, welcoming me back to work. He apologized for what he had put me through and thanked me for helping his girlfriend in a time of need. He promised to give me the best tables to serve from then on. I suggested he should invite Dr. Jamal for dinner, in appreciation for helping save his girlfriend's life. I had an open account and promised to chip in with the bill. Dr. Jamal was flattered by the invitation. He was allowed to invite whomever he wanted. He and his friends were served the best steaks, wine, and desserts on the house. Michael had the opportunity to once again thank him. Brenda welcomed me back to work with open arms, and she also had the opportunity to personally thank the doctor for saving her life.

I have learned that we never realize how precious life is until we lose a loved one or come close to losing our own life. Life can be unpredictable. A human life is not supposed to be taken for granted. Sometimes, Michael would ask me if I could ever forgive him for what he had put me through I let him know all was forgiven. He will never know the emotional pain I endured due to his harassment.

I found the time to also invite David and his colleague for dinner at the inn to thank them for being there for me when I needed a shoulder to cry on. My memories of almost losing my life never leave me. You are aware that you're a little different from your friends. Regardless of how hard you try to blend in with the crowd, there seems to be a higher power that tends to guard your every move from getting in with the crowd.

chapter 14

As I was heading out the door, I heard on the radio that there was an outcry from the public, complaining about how the homeless people were being treated in the emergency room. They complained that they would be there for hours and would not be seen by a doctor. I said to Mom that they have a right to complain because they have a voice, but most important, they are human beings. As time went on, we didn't hear officials addressing the matter, and we assumed the homeless people were forgotten. It was not important, just another story making headline news. At the hospital, I had to work the midnight shift alone again. The other telephone operator had called in sick. Before we sat in front of the board, we usually had to clean our headsets and chairs with rubbing alcohol. It was very important for us to do so, especially at nights. The supervisor always advised us that even though there's security at the gate, we should always be careful, especially working at nights. It was my second night in a row working the 10:00 p.m. to 7:00 a.m. shift, and I couldn't wait to get some sleep.

It was a Friday night, and having seen the schedule, I realized I wouldn't make it to the inn and had to let the manager know. Instead of telling me it was okay, he insisted on me coming in at whatever time I got relieved. I was a very appreciative of that. Sometimes it was tough juggling two jobs with different schedules, but God always opened a way for me to make it. Except for the one incident, the manager let me know he had confidence in me. He always showed respect, integrity, and dignity to the other employees and me. He was a good boss after all.

It was around midnight on this particular Friday night, while working the midnight shift alone once again, when I heard a loud knock at the door. I hesitated for a moment. Then again there was a knock, and this time it sounded with a sense of urgency. I cautiously walked up the stairs and slightly moved the curtain that covered the glass. Standing in the front of the door was a middle-aged, tall gentleman with a torn hat and clothes. I slightly opened the door and asked the gentleman if I could help him. The well-spoken, homeless-looking gentleman, who didn't have a pleasant odor, asked me if I could help him find a doctor. I politely told him he'd have to go back to the emergency room and have the nurse call me to get in touch with the doctor on call. He told me the nurses were being disrespectful to him, and he was concerned if his nephew didn't see a doctor soon, he may not make it. I followed my intuition and asked the gentleman to come in. I thought maybe, just maybe, he had fallen on hard times. Even though it was the nurse's responsibility to call me, I was concerned for the gentleman's nephew.

I paged the doctor on call, who had just gone in to have his lunch at that hour. He was the only doctor on call in the emergency room that night. I explained the situation to him and humbly asked him if he could help the gentleman. Instead of allowing the gentleman to stand, I asked him to have a seat and use the courtesy phone. Dr. Edwards took the necessary information from the gentleman and advised him to return the emergency room, saying he would be right there. I thanked Dr. Edwards for being courteous and asked him to let me know how everything worked out. The gentleman thanked me and returned to the emergency room as advised. Several hours later, I learned had the patient waited one more minute, he would have died from internal bleeding. I felt relieved to know he was going to be all right.

The following morning when I left work, before returning home, I went into the cathedral and thanked God for protecting me throughout the night, giving me the strength and courage to follow my intuition to help the gentleman. When I returned home, I confided in Mom what had happened. A heavy burden had been lifted from me by having to make a split decision about whether to turn the gentleman away, referring him back to the nurse, or take the initiative myself. The expression on his face and the desperate pleading in his voice mattered more than what he was wearing. Mom told me I made the right choice. Had the young man died, it would have certainly been on my conscience for the rest of my life. Dr. Edwards didn't have to take me seriously; he could have told me it was the nurse's responsibility to have him paged. Instead, he did listen to me and took the call seriously. Because of my response, I was able to help save the life of a patient that night.

I was off from the hospital for the weekend, and I was finally able to get some sleep. Later on that evening when I returned to work, I felt comfortable working at the inn again. There was no time for me to socialize. I often silently dreamed that someday the situation would get better and I could study family law. I always had a passion for family law. I only discussed this with Mom. She would advise me to continue to aim for what I wanted in life, to hold on to my dream and never let it go. Ask God for my heart's desire. If it is his will, thy will be done; if not, he will show me a sign along the way if I'm on the right path. Otherwise, except the fact it may not be my calling. Mom reminded me to continue to trust and believe in God, and to turn my burdens over to him.

When I return to work at the hospital, the supervisor told me there was a call for me from the minister's secretary. She said she'd call back, which she did. I wondered why she wanted to speak with me. After verifying who I was, she said the minister wished to speak to me. She then connected me to him. When he was through with his greeting, he asked me how the patient's condition was. I politely asked him which patient he was he referring to. He said he wished to see me in his office, it was important. He further stated he needed to know if I could come in the said day; he would arrange for security clearance for me. I told him I'd try my best to come in. I was uncertain as to what this was all about. I confided in my colleague and best friend, Agnes, who advised me to go because that was the only way I would find out what it was all about. She further stated that not every citizen had the opportunity to see a figure of authority, especially that particular minister in person. I called back to verify that I would come in as soon as I got relieved. On my way to the office, I silently prayed that I was not in trouble for the decision that I had made. After all, it was not the right procedure. The call was supposed to come in directly from the nurse.

When I arrived at the ministry, I was ushered into the minister's office. On the wall were pictures of dignitaries from around the world. As I stood nervously facing the gentleman, I wondered to myself, *how did I get here?* After officially introducing himself, he said, "You're wondering why I asked you to come in." I politely replied, "Yes, sir!" His voice sounded familiar, but from where? He then asked me, "Did you help the gentleman that came to the operator's booth on Friday night to find a doctor?" I asked him how he knew about that. He looked directly into my eyes and said, "I was that person." I was dumbfounded. Feeling tricked, I asked him why he was dressed in that manner. He said because of the numerous complaints they were getting in regards to how the members of the public, including the homeless, were being treated in the emergency room by the nurses, he and other officials went undercover to investigate. While there, word came in on the walkie-talkie that the ambulance was bringing in his nephew. Having been there for quite some time without any assistance, in desperation, he came to the operator's booth seeking help. He further stated he got a firsthand experience of what the homeless people were experiencing. He thanked me for helping him find a doctor to help save his nephew's life and for treating him in a dignified manner.

I asked him how he knew my name. He said it was his responsibility to know all the citizens' names, especially civil servants. He then reached over to his desk and handed me two complimentary tickets to attend the Miss Universe Reception. He said it was in appreciation for treating him with dignity. I could bring anyone I wanted to. I could not believe it. I thanked him and slowly walked out of the office and headed for the cathedral. I cried for the homeless people and for those who were not being treated in the manner they deserved. I prayed that my family and I may never have to be in that situation. I thanked God for giving me the courage to help the gentleman.

When I arrived home, I showed my sister Mindy the tickets and invited her, but she declined. Mom was visiting her mother in Grenada, who had returned from Venezuela for the first time since leaving her at a tender age. I then invited Mitch, and he made a fuss of not wanting to attend. He had gotten promoted and was transferred to the Intelligence Bureau. He had taken an oath never to discuss his line of work, not even with his mother. That made him very cautious about everything. Meanwhile, he was taking a course in photography at the university.

The public fell in love with Miss Universe from the night she won the competition. As word began to spread of the big event in her honor, everybody wanted to get a glimpse of the most beautiful woman in the universe. It was said on the news that there was going to be very tight security at the reception that was going to be held in her honor. It was headline news around the country. As the time drew near, Mitch finally agreed to attend with me. On the day of the event, Mindy made sure we were dressed for the special occasion. When we arrived at the venue, the streets were lined with a lot of people waiting behind bars, under tight security, to get a glimpse of Miss Universe. As we were about to enter the compound, there were shouts of "Give us your tickets!" The female officer looked at us from head to toe and said, "Tickets please." Mitch proudly said, "Sure." She then smiled and said to enjoy ourselves.

As soon as we were led into the reception hall, Mitch began snapping away at all the dignitaries, including Miss Universe. She was very beautiful in person. He only stopped for a brief moment to have a drink. We enjoyed ourselves very much. It was a beautiful evening. Later, I asked Mitch why he didn't take a picture of me with Miss Universe or other dignitaries, and he said he got carried away. I felt very disappointed because it was an experience of a lifetime to remember. However, I still had the memories. He did a magnificent job taking those beautiful pictures. Most of his colleagues wanted to know how he got so close to Miss Universe. He was delighted to have had the opportunity to have met her. They began to respect him even more.

Shortly after the investigation, unfortunately several nurses lost their jobs. A lot of changes were made. There was more than one doctor assigned to the emergency room, especially on weekends, and also in the operating room. Upon Mom's return, she was proud to know we had attended the special gala of a lifetime, but she was upset at Mitch for not taking a picture of me along with some of the guests. She didn't forget to give him a good lecture.

Mom never stopped praying for her children, and our safety. She always reminded us, regardless of how busy we are, to always remember to thank God for the gift of life, along with his many special blessings that he has bestowed upon us. She would advise us to never take anything in life for granted, because in life there are no guarantees. We are here today, and in a split second could be gone tomorrow. Mom was right in saying this to us. I received a call from my friend Lela informing me her sister had died. Her mother, upon hearing the news of Lela's sister's death, collapsed and went into cardiac arrest. Unfortunately, Lela's Mom died. She was devastated. I tried my best to give her words of inspiration. How can we emotionally handle the sudden death of our loved ones? Frist comes the anger of asking yourself why this had to happen. It's followed by the sorrow and sadness, dealing with the deep emotional pain and wondering if God really and truly does exist in heaven. We have to sincerely believe he's there and knows what we're going through. Only he has the answer and knows best. All we can do is continue to hold onto our faith, keep our Bibles close to our heart, and cry out to him to help heal our broken soul, mind, body, and spirit. In due time, hopefully the emotional pain will get a little easier to bear. Only he holds the answer to why it happens to our loved ones and not ourselves.

One of the things I admired about Mitch was he was always a cool, calm, and collected person. He never boasted of his accomplishments. He would surprise Mom with a trophy he won in table tennis or medals he would receive in some other sporting event on behalf of the army. Sometimes we would be invited to attend one of the sporting games between the soldiers and police officers, air force, or coast guards. We would have a good laugh at how competitive those guys were with each other, trying to win. One of the challenges that Mitch had to face—which he never told Mom about in order not to upset her—was when law enforcement officers were sent in search of one of the most wanted fugitives, who was armed and dangerous. It was on the news. A mother's intuition knows when one of her children is facing some kind of trouble. Mom suddenly got down on her knees and began to pray for the protection and safety of Mitch. With tears streaming down her face, she began to cry out to God to protect him from whatever dangerous situation he was about to encounter, along with the other officers. Mom was not only feeling her child's fears, but the realization of what he was about to encounter. We were all scared, and my nephew and I joined Mom in prayer, pleading with God to protect Mitch wherever he was.

One of his colleagues told me that Mitch was one of the officers sent in search of the fugitive, and they didn't know how long they would be gone. I was advised not to mention anything to Mom, in fear that she would worry herself sick. I couldn't let her know. We all kept on praying that God would continue to guide and protect him and the other law enforcement officers. Weeks had gone by, and there was no word about catching the fugitive. Finally, I received a call from his colleague letting me know that the search was over. Mitch had apprehended the suspect. He said the suspect, who was armed, had come down from the hills to drink water from a stand pipe. When his head was down drinking the water, Mitch identified himself to him and told him he was surrounded, to drop his weapon. He refused, and Mitch went on tell him he didn't want to have to shoot him down like an animal, to throw down his weapon and raise his hands in the air. His colleague went on to tell me that it took some time for Mitch to finally convince him to give up peacefully without being shot down. The fugitive finally surrendered. The way Mom raised us, believing there's a solution to every problem, without using violence, never left our minds. Being a Christian, Mitch had to use his wisdom and try not to shoot the fugitive. His friend Bret told me it took him quite a while, trying to convince the fugitive to stand up as a man and owe up to the responsibility for committing such heinous crimes. Bret further stated it was on the news and in the newspaper. I had to read it for myself to believe it. Mom heard it on the radio, and the neighbors across the street brought the article from the newspaper for her to read. When I arrived home later on that day, Mom was praying at the altar, giving praise and glory to God for bringing Mitch and the other officers home safely, without any bloodshed.

The precinct was not far from where we lived. Officer Paul and I were best friends, and he was aware that we didn't have a telephone. He was one of the officers that would come to our home to relay the message from the hospital or the Service Commission, to let me know when or where they needed me to work next when my assignment was completed at the hospital. Before I could rest my head, I would be called back in to work at the hospital or at some other ministry. Paul was aware I was not street smart. He would take the time to let me know of the latest dangerous drugs that were circulating the country and would advise me on how to protect myself from being drugged in any way. I appreciated that very much.

He had come from a large family and was the main bread winner. He was helping to send his sisters to private school. Meanwhile, his father was serving time for a crime he didn't commit. Paul was street smart and also a very strict cop. Everybody in the district was afraid of him; he was a no-nonsense person, but he was good cop. He was promoted to detective and invited my family and me to his wedding. His sisters had finally completed their education and were doing well for themselves. Unfortunately, on that beautiful Sunday, I was assigned to volunteer with the other members of the Red Cross at the beach.

Both he and his beautiful wife went swimming in the bay. The waters were very rough. Unfortunately, he had gotten himself with difficulties in the water. We tried desperately to save his life. Sadly, he died on his way to the hospital. I had lost a good friend who had always showed me utmost respect and tried to protect me the best way he knew how. The day before he died, the truth was finally revealed of his father's innocence. After spending several years in jail, his father was out in time to see his son buried. He took on the role of a father to help his large family of ten on an officer's salary. He often confided in me how tough it was for him to even support himself. Mom would invite him over from time to time to have lunch or dinner. On the night of his wake, the police apprehended thieves who broke into a warehouse not far from his home.

His wife gave birth to a beautiful healthy boy. He didn't live to see his only child grow into a fine young man and later became a prison officer. However, I'm sure he's in heaven smiling down at his family. Words cannot express how deeply sad I felt after he died. The district was never the same after his death. Before he died, there was always law and order. The youths were on their best behavior. No crimes were being committed. After his death, the youths began to run wild, committing crime after crime until another cop, tougher than he was, was sent to restore law and order.

chapter 15

Dad still found the time to write to us whenever he felt like it, but Mitch was not interested in communicating with him anymore. There was too much emotional turmoil deep within his soul, which could not be erased. Even though Dad took Mom for granted, she stood by him. She hung in there and didn't quit. Dad eventually died. Mom was there to see that he had a decent burial. One of the things I'll always love Dad for was that he gave Mom respect. Even though he was aware she had two children from previous relationships that ended in heartbreak, he married her. Back then, few men married women with children from different relationships. They were looked down on as "used goods."

Mindy and I have different opinions about the topic. She doesn't understand how some women feel, not getting the respect they so highly deserve. I've had a few friends who were in similar situations. I stood by their side through the emotional turmoil they were faced with and silently prayed I wouldn't ever find myself in that situation. One of my friends, Nathalie, had two children from different relationships. Her mother had died giving birth to her. She grew up with her grandmother, who helped raise the children. She told me of the handsome guy she was seeing. She talked about how well he was treating her. She was unemployed at the time, and he was a civil servant holding a good position. I advised her to take it slow, but I guess she got caught up with his sweet talk. She fell for it. It was not long after they began seeing each other, she got pregnant. He then began to give her the cold shoulder. He was no longer helping her financially. She felt helpless. I promised her I'd try my best to stand by her side until she found a job.

One day, I told Mom that after I left work at the hospital, I was going to visit my friend. She knew I was helping her financially, and she didn't object. When I arrived at her home, there was a confrontation between my friend and the father of the baby. He had stopped by unexpectedly. She found out he was seeing someone else, who was also a civil servant, and she was waiting in his car. They got into an argument, and he decided to walk away. Instead of leaving it alone, she armed herself with an object and began to follow him, with me in pursuit, pleading with her to come back, to think of the baby and throw away the object. She didn't hear what I had to say. Instead of taking the main road, he took a shortcut, trying to get away from her. Meanwhile, she was cussing and being emotional. I was concerned that she could hurt herself or the baby. She was already seven months pregnant. Having rained the night before, the hills were slippery, and he was way ahead of her, but that didn't stop her from pursuing him. I fell into a pool of mud and screamed, letting her know I'd had it with her. She stopped and turned around. It was there and then that I realized when a woman is pregnant, depending on the emotional situation she's faced with, she can temporarily lose her mind. I was in mud from head to toe and very upset with her for putting me in that position. Her grandmother had pleaded with me to try to stop her from finding herself in trouble, seeing she already had two young ones who were depending on her. Then and there, I let her have it. I reminded her what guys do. Because she has a good figure, they make her believe she's the one and the only one, promising her the world, which they don't mean. They wait until they get what they want from her, and then their true colors come out. I had to take a shower and change into one of her oversized outfits to return home. Before leaving, I gave her the envelope I had brought for her, along with a few gifts for the baby.

When I arrived home, my nephew came rushing to the door, wanting to know why I was dressed like that. Children are very observant. They watch everything and need answers right away. He then called out to Mom to have a look at my outfit. Nathalie and I were in the same unit together. I continued to help her, but I was cautious about visiting her at home. She asked me to be the baby's godmother. I was delighted to do so. Today my godson is a striving young man. I helped her get a job. Today, she has her own home and holds a good position. The child's father got married to his newfound love.

One bright and sunny day, when I returned home from work, Mom said to me, "You will never believe who was here." I told her I didn't know, and she asked me to make a guess. I told her I couldn't guess. She said the minister was there with his nephew, who had come in from London to be with the other nephew during his recovery. I was shocked. She said he told her what had happened and he wanted to compliment her on the way she raised me. I asked her how he got my address. Mom said that in his position, he could easily find out.

Uncle Randolph came in from London on a short visit. Mom got up the following morning and told him of a dream she had. She advised him to be very careful. She told him she saw someone put something in his meal, and she didn't see him again in the dream. He then told her he had come to attend a function in his honor, given by an ex-classmate. They had both been up for a scholarship, which Uncle Randolph had won. Mom advised him not to go. She was able to give a good description of the person she saw in her dream who had put whatever it was in his meal. Uncle Randolph told her the description she gave him was that of his friend. However, being a medical doctor, he didn't believe in dreams. Before leaving, Mom pleaded with him not to attend the function. Nevertheless, he still went, promising to be careful.

During the night, Mom suddenly woke up. She was emotional, looking through the window. I also got up. I asked her what was wrong. She said she had an unusual feeling something had happened to Uncle Randolph. We were unable to go back to sleep. Rover began to howl very loudly with her head toward the sky. We knew someone in the family was going to die. Rover had howled like that right before Lenny died. Mom was still up looking through the window with her flashlight. Suddenly, Rover began to bark. Mom got concerned when her younger brother came instead of Uncle Randolph. Unfortunately, he told her Uncle Randolph had died. He had taken ill at the party and was rushed to the hospital. The hardest thing he had to do was inform my uncle's wife for her to break the news to their young son. It was later confirmed he had died from "food poisoning." His body was flown back to London for the burial.

We were always very careful whenever Mom said she had a dream. Mindy would say she was tired of hearing Mom's dreams. I'm sure that upset Mom, but she never said anything to her. Being the first child, Mom loved her unconditionally. In her eyes, she could do no wrong. The day finally came when Mom warned her of a particular dream. She didn't listen to Mom, until she got her heart broken. She fell on her knees and asked Mom to forgive her for not believing in her dreams. Mom would tell us, the Lord said, "Before he destroys a city, he will send a messenger to warn us." She would say that the Lord chose her to be the messenger to warn us whenever there was danger or heart break around the corner. All she would ask of us was to take heed. Lenny once had warned Mindy of a prediction, and she told him she didn't want to hear it. It wasn't long after the conversation, I overheard Mom telling Lenny how right he was. What he had warned her about had come true.

chapter 16

M y assignments were finally over, and it was time for me to start a new chapter of my life. Before leaving Trinidad, I told the manager of the inn about my departure. At the airport, my friend Agnes told me the manager was travelling on the same flight with me. She said she saw him board the same aircraft. I told her maybe she made a mistake. To my surprise, when I arrived at JFK, we met face-to-face. He shook my hand and wished me the best. He was in transit to Florida.

Five years later, my sister sent word that I had gotten a permanent position at the hospital. I couldn't turn back. Mom always told us that with God, nothing happens before its time.

To the medical residents, we are aware that you are young and handsome and want to get ahead. I strongly urge you, don't do it at the expense of the patients. They are not guinea pigs. They are human beings, whom God has created just like you. They may not have the same profession as you, but there's absolutely no need to prescribe medication for a patient who's not your patient because you assume they may need it. Consult with the patient's primary physician before doing so. Talk to the patient and explain why you are prescribing that particular medication for them. Please remember patients have rights to accept or not to accept the medication you have prescribed. Let the patient be aware of the serious side effects of the medication. Advise them, should there be any unusual changes in their body, to consult their doctor or return to the hospital immediately. Don't run and hide when the patient returns to your office with complaints. Please remember you have taken an oath to care for the sick and suffering. You are not invisible, you are not God, and if you are not cautious, you will certainly find yourself in legal trouble. Take your time in diagnosing a patient. Do your job to the best of your abilities. You are not running a competition; you are dealing with real people. Who on earth do you think you are? You make your hospital rounds with your superior, and when you get to the patient's bed, you stare them down like they are shit! God has chosen you for this calling. Please do it with dignity. Otherwise, you may not even complete your studies because he sees the wrong you do to some patients, laughing about it when you think no one is watching or listening to you. When you take an oath to care for the sick and suffering, is it the dollar signs you see?

Please avoid being cruel to the sick and suffering, and don't you dare do it in a slick way and think no one is watching you. Please avoid being cruel to the helpless and vulnerable patients that have been entrusted into your care. The patients that are coming to see you at the hospital or at your private practice are the ones that are helping to pay your salary. The day the patients stop coming to your hospital or practice, you will have to close down. Remember, God gives each and every one of us a chance to redeem ourselves. If you continue to do wrong and think you are higher than him, he will definitely strike you down when you least expect it. He's watching your every move. Please do the right thing. Let it be a new beginning for you.

To all the good doctors and nurses, continue to do the outstanding job that God has chosen you to do. You'll be amazed at the many wonderful blessings that he will bestow upon you and your family, all because you are doing the right things in his eyes by caring for the sick and suffering, the lame and the weak, giving them hope and a reason to stay alive.

To doctors, please be advised before you admit a child or an adult into the isolation ward. Have several tests done first. Before you admit the patient into that ward, explain to the parties involved how cold the temperature is in there so they know what to expect. They are human beings. Treat the patients as you would like your colleagues to treat your elderly parents or grandparents. Also remember, you are not going to remain young and handsome forever. You will grow old someday, and you will want to be treated in a dignified manner. Remember what goes around comes around, and you will certainly reap what you sow.

Should you have a loved one admitted to the isolation ward, please make sure before their release from the hospital, an X-ray is taken to show they do not have pneumonia. Have the attending physician show you the X-ray and read it to you in layman terms. Should you find your loved one have a wheezing sound, take your loved one immediately back to the hospital. Time is of the essence. Please don't take any chances. If your loved one is not attended to immediately, they can slip in and out of consciousness and will have to be placed on life support. I sincerely hope and pray no other parent ever has to go through what I experienced with my child due to someone else's negligence.

chapter 17

Shortly before I left home, I met a young man who claimed he was interested in taking me out. I explained to him I was engaged and could not go out with him. A few months later, when I visited my uncle, he said he would like me to meet his good friend. When I walked into the living room, as my uncle introduced us, standing in front of me was the young man who wanted to take me out. He then asked my uncle, "Is this really your niece?" He went on to tell him he had asked me out and I gave him a difficult time. My uncle said, "You give guys a hard time? I'm proud of you." Life is unpredictable. We have to be aware there are no guarantees in life. It can take you places you never dream off. We sometimes don't have an answer for everything that happens in our lives. We can only trust and believe there's a higher power, along with his angels, watching and protecting our every move. Depending on the life we live, he'll show us answers in due time to our burning questions.

Whenever I returned from work, if I left the light off, when I returned, the light would be on. If I left it on, upon my return, it would be off. I spoke to my cousin Albert, who was the owner. He checked the fuses and said there wasn't a problem. He advised me, should I continue to experience the problem, to let him know. I didn't experience the problem again. On a beautiful Saturday morning, I decided to visit my aunt. As I patiently waited for the train, I had a strong intuition to return home. I tried to ignore the feeling, but it was strong, so I had to act on it. As I slowly walked home, I silently prayed that God would protect me from whatever danger lay ahead of me. I had no idea what to expect, and I sure didn't like how I was feeling. When I arrived home, after I unlooked the two locks leading inside, I wondered why I had strong intuition to return home. There was no one in the hallway, and it was very quiet as I slowly walked toward my apartment. As I stood in front of the door, there seem to be something wrong with the door. Mom used to always warn us to always check our doors before we go out. Be sure that when we return, we find it the same way we left it. As I stood there, the feelings began to get stronger. Instead of unlocking the door, I turned the handle and was shocked when the door almost came off my hand. I looked inside and couldn't believe my eyes. Sitting on my couch smoking was one of the tenants on my floor. Upon seeing me, he dashed out of my apartment, almost knocking me down. I was shaken up. I immediately called my cousin. I called the police, and the trespasser was arrested. However, I was advised by the police to try to move out before he got out. They said it was not a safe environment for me to live in. Fortunately, I was able to move out before he was released. I began to notice I was having strong intuitions about certain things, and I couldn't explain why. Mom once told me I had a gift and she wanted me to always follow my intuition.

Upon my return to Trinidad, my friends surprised me when they took me to dinner at the inn where I used to work. Instead of serving the guests, I was served by my friend, the maître de, and the head waiter. It was a beautiful experience seeing my ex-coworkers again, who let me know "you never miss the water until the well runs dry." It was indeed a beautiful evening.

Shortly after I returned to New York, I had a strong intuition something was going to happen to me. I couldn't explain it. My sister had spent the night with me and was returning to her destination. She asks me what was wrong, and I told her how I felt. She advised me not to come with her, but I was concerned because it was her first visit to

New York. When we arrived at her destination, she asked how I was feeling. I told her the feelings were getting stronger and I needed to get off the streets. She then advised me to call a friend to accompany me back home, which I did.

I called my friend Brad, whom I had known for a while and who was also from my hometown. I told him how I was feeling. He told me not to leave until he came to meet me. When he finally arrived, he said his car was at the mechanic's. I told him I'd pay for a cab. He insisted, "It's a beautiful evening, let's take the bus." I didn't want to argue with him; I just wanted to get off the streets. While on our way home, it rained. I noticed that whenever rain falls, it doesn't matter what time it is, you seldom see anyone on the streets. As soon as we got off the bus, I noticed a short guy walking down the street with a fast pace; he seemed to be looking for an easy target. I drew my friend's attention and suggested we cross over. When I turned around, the young man was close behind us. I suggested we cross back to the other side, and as we did so, the guy whistled. We didn't think anything of it at the time. Brad was walking with his head down. As we continued to walk, the feelings began getting stronger. I silently reached out to God and all the saints in heaven to protect us. Pleading with him, if we have to die, don't let us die a terrible death on the street. When I looked down, I noticed a very tall shadow next to mine. I then felt heavy breathing at the side of my neck. I gave a slight glimpse over my shoulder and saw a tall guy close to me. I thought he wanted to pass by. I turned around and said, "Oh excuse me."

Meanwhile, my pocketbook just kept on dangling from off my shoulder. When I raised my head again, I couldn't believe it. There were six guys standing there with their hands in their pockets, including the short guy. I felt frozen. Brad continued walking. I then heard one of the guys say, "Get him! Get him!" Two of them ran up to Brad and grabbed him. One locked his neck and placed a knife to his throat, while the other patted him down. When they realized they didn't find anything, the one holding the knife burst the chain from off his neck, and they ran off. The remaining four just stood there staring at me as I slightly turned my head, not wanting to stare directly at them. Regardless of how we are trained to defend ourselves, when you are faced with muggers, you are frozen. I then heard a loud horn began blowing. One of the guys snatched my pocketbook and ran off. The others followed. A gentleman was sitting in his car on the same side of the street, a little further up. He had seen what happened and began to blow his horn to scare off the muggers. The landlord, who didn't live on the premises, happened to be there that night doing some work in the basement. I was lucky he was there to open the doors for me. My keys were in my pocketbook.

My friend Florence said how lucky we were, because that same night, her neighbor had gotten mugged and was shot to death. She couldn't understand how we didn't get hurt, being surrounded by six guys. I said to her, "I wish I had an answer for that question, but I don't. Only God has the answer." Florence and I had been good friends for over five years. Even though she was from Aruba, she had relatives living in Curacao. We always had something interesting to talk about. It was on that day while talking to her, I became concerned by her heavy breathing. I asked her if she had run to come to the phone, and she said no. I advised her to see her physician as soon as possible for a routine checkup. Her breathing didn't sound normal.

The next day, she told me she was going in to see her physician and would call me when she returned. Later that evening, when I didn't hear from her, I called and was told by her brother that she was admitted to the hospital because of the swelling of both feet. I kept in touch with her, and when I couldn't visit her at the hospital, I would ask about her condition. I was told she was improving and would be released shortly. A particular night, I was doing the dishes when I had the intuition to call her. I decided to wait until I was through to call, but the feelings were strong, so I had to act on it. The person who answered the phone wanted to know who was calling. There was lot of laughter in the background. I thought for a minute maybe they were celebrating her release from the hospital. When her brother came to the phone, I was shocked when he said Florence had died and she would be buried the following morning. I was unable to say anything for a few minutes. Through my tears, I tried to ask, "How? When?" I didn't get much sleep that night. Unfortunately, everything went wrong the following morning with traffic on the road; it seemed as though it was not meant to be. When I finally arrived, I was told the hearse had just left. I was very emotional. It took me some time to get over her death.

Recently, my aunt asked me if I had ESP (Extra Sensory Perception). She said whenever she's about to call me, I always call her instead. I cannot answer that question for sure, but I have learned to follow that unusual feeling that I get from time to time. I guess it's something we all have within us, only sometimes we find ourselves too busy to pay attention to it. Please try to always follow your intuition. I look at it as God's way of giving us a signal.

Due to an injury, I was on a particular pain medication. After a while, I began experiencing tightness in my chest, nausea, pain radiating from my shoulder straight down to my arm, vomiting, and blackouts. My physician began to monitor me on regular basics. It was very uncomfortable for me, especially the tightness in my chest. I silently prayed that God would help me find the answer as to why was I having those symptoms regularly. At some point, even my wrist had begun turning in, as though I was getting a stroke. The doctor couldn't find the answers. There were no other medical conditions, and everything was normal except for the signs and symptoms that I was getting on a regular basis.

One day, as I sat on the couch reading the newspaper, the fly that had been around since after Lenny's death was on the article I was reading. I noticed that whenever anything bad is going to happen the following day, the fly is always around. There's a friend that I had always trusted throughout the years. The day before her visits, the fly would suddenly appear, flying around in a hurry. I couldn't understand it. Even during her visits, it would fly around in our presence with such speed. I believe my brother's spirit was trying to tell me something from beyond. I had to try to understand what was happening. I began to pay close attention. Something wasn't right, but what was it? I finally found out the truth. The person that I had trusted throughout the years was a wolf in sheep's clothing. I've learned we have to be aware of what's going on not only in our lives, but also with our children, our surroundings, and in and around our home. Otherwise, we're not living; we're only existing. Mom always told us that God speaks to us in parables. He sends his angels to warn us when there's danger around. Mom wanted us to have the knowledge and the wisdom to walk by faith and not by sight.

As I sat there, I silently asked God to protect us from whatever danger lay ahead of us. The fly left the article and flew around and on me, even resting on my chest. It seemed to be giving some kind of blessing. I took this very seriously. Throughout the night, it didn't fly away; instead it rested on the ceiling over my bed. I had absolutely no idea what was about to transpire in less than twenty-four hours.

The following morning when I awoke, the fly was gone. My daughter said she wasn't feeling well. She had a high temperature. She just wanted a glass of orange juice. I made her some homemade chicken soup and then administered the medication to her, as prescribed by her pediatrician. Shortly thereafter, she fell asleep. I sat on the chair at the foot of the bed and proceeded to write. I checked my daughter's respiration in between, and it was beating normally. I seldom wear my diamond ring—I hadn't worn it in three years—but I decided to wear it that day. I had spoken to Mom earlier, trying to gather as much information as I possibly could about Grandma and Grandpa. Mom was aware that I was doing this to honor her, for how hard she toiled from sunrise to sunset to ensure our needs were met.

At 7: 00 p.m., before having dinner, I checked on my daughter. She was sleeping so peacefully. After I placed the dinner on the tray, I had some cranberry juice, and then I went back into the bedroom and sat on the chair. After I had the first scoop, I said to myself, "I didn't know I could cook this well." The meal sure tasted delicious.

I never anticipated for one minute that may have been the last meal I prepared. As I was about to have the second scoop, I suddenly felt a sharp, excruciating, explosive pain in my heart. My whole body shook. I actually felt my heart pitch to the right side of my chest. It felt as though someone had stabbed me directly in my heart with a sharp instrument. I thought I may have pulled a muscle, even though I was aware that the signs and symptoms were that of a heart attack. I didn't want to accept the fact. As I sat there waiting for the pain to subside, I saw a bright light, so bright that it dazzled my eyesight. I blinked my eyes, and the light was still there. I closed my eyes and silently believed God knew what I wanted. When I opened my eyes, the light was still there, it was so very bright. I couldn't even see my hands, my child lying on the bed, the ring, much less the diamond on the ring. I felt very weak and scared. I felt I was going to die.

Suddenly, I felt an inner peace come over me, one that I have never experience before. Everything seemed so calm, so still, so very still. I didn't feel scared anymore. I was ready to die.

That's when I felt myself sliding down from of the chair. At first it started slowly, gradually, and then it picked up with a fast pace. I realized my daughter would get up and find me dead on the floor. With my hand clutching my heart, I tried desperately to apply pressure to my heart, but I wasn't doing it hard enough. I realized I only had seconds or minutes before I dropped dead. I was going down faster and faster. I felt I wasn't going to make it. I felt so very weak. I had to keep trying. It was a physical fight to help save my life, for the love of my child and myself. I jabbed my hand into my heart, with whatever strength I had remaining, and began to press as hard as I possibly could, without stopping to count one-two-three. I believe God gave me the strength and the courage to apply pressure hard to my heart. Slowly, my breathing came back. When I opened my eyes, the light was gone, but I couldn't say my name. The words wouldn't come out. I looked at my daughter sleeping soundly, unaware of the traumatic experience I'd just had. I didn't want to wake and alarm her with a sign stating that I couldn't talk and to call an ambulance. I looked at the telephone and wondered if I pressed the speed dial button to 911, if the operator would take the call seriously, guessing that the party on the other line had a medical crisis and was unable to respond to his or her questions. I slowly wrote on a legal pad, "To Whom It May Concern," indicating in case of my sudden death, who should have custody of my child, and where all my important documents were, and to give my good organs to whomever may be in need of them. Reality was staring me in the face. I was not sure I was going to make it through the night. When I was through writing, I drank the remaining cranberry juice. I slowly picked up the tray, headed for the kitchen, and disposed the rest of the meal. I then slowly went into the bathroom, washed my hands, and got a glimpse of myself in the mirror. I almost didn't recognize myself.

My face looked very pale, and the pupils of my eyes didn't look good. In other words, I looked like death. Each step I took seemed to be the last. I slowly walked back into the room, sat down on the chair, and silently prayed. God had brought me this far, and I believed that he would see me through the night. I couldn't say a word. I felt very weak. As I curled up in the chair, my hand was not too far from my heart, should the pain come back. The next thing I knew, my daughter woke me up the following morning at 6:00 a.m. She wanted to know what was wrong. Why was I sleeping on the chair and with the same clothes on? I was able to respond to her. I explained to her what happened while she was asleep and that I would have to go to the hospital. After taking her temperature, I saw that it was back to normal. I told her to go over to her grandmother's home after school. According to the situation, the nurse would call her grandmother. Before leaving, I prepared dinner just in case her aunt had to come and get her clothes. I moved around very slowly. Even though my daughter slept in the master bedroom, I made sure her bed was properly made. I then slowly walked into the bathroom and had a shower. I had to hold onto the bar for fear of falling.

I felt like I wasn't going to be physically returning home. Instead of calling for an ambulance, I decided to take public transportation to enjoy the beautiful scenery just one more time. At the time, it felt like the right thing to do. It didn't cross my mind I was losing whatever little oxygen I had remaining in my heart. As I headed for the hospital, just the scent of baked fish made me nauseous. I had to get to the hospital quickly. As soon as I arrived at the hospital, as I was about to sign in, I collapsed. I began to slip in and out of consciousness. I heard the doctor ask me what medication I was on. I was able to tell him, and I then heard him say he couldn't find a pulse. I could hear more than one person in the room. They were talking about my heart rate. They could barely get a beat, and my respiration had dropped. My life was in God's hands.

I heard the doctor say something about the trauma room. I've never been in a trauma room before. In there, it was very scary. To me, being in there is close to death. I don't remember everything after, except hearing someone speaking loudly. She wanted to know what I was thinking. She went onto say I had a lack of oxygen flow to my heart. She continued to check the computer. I cannot say how much longer after I was told I had to have a cat scan. The doctor needed to know if any damage was done to my brain. Thank God, no damage was done. On the day I was admitted, I had an appointment to see my physician. Prior to the traumatic experience, I had come across an article in the newspaper that said researchers found that cranberry juice was not only good to fight and help prevent urinary tract infection, but it was also good for the immune system, including the brain. I believe that drinking the remaining cranberry juice may have helped to prevent any damage to my brain.

I was awakened by the loud sobs coming from my daughter as she rested her head on my chest, pleading with me not to die, saying her life would never be the same without me. I felt very weak as I simply patted her back, reassuring her that my life was in God's hands and I had no control over my destiny. As she continued to sob, the nurse walked into the room to see if everything was all right. It was then I learned, after she helped raise my daughter off my chest, that the device that was hooked up to my heart was attached to the computer to monitor my heart rate. It had shifted, and she had to readjust it. The nurse had called Mom to let her know I was admitted. My daughter, upon learning I was admitted, left school during recess to visit me at the hospital. I was upset with her for not being at school, but when she said to me, "Mom, I cannot remain focused while you're in the hospital," I understood her fears. I couldn't stay upset with her for long. After all, I almost didn't get a chance to say good-bye to her. I had to appreciate every second I had with her. Time was very precious.

Every day during recess, she would come to visit me. She would get emotional seeing me hooked up to the oxygen and the rest that goes with it. I needed her to be strong for whatever life presented to us, and it sure didn't look good at the time. I was about to be taken for a test, and I began to feel very dizzy. I told the nurse how I felt. She advised the ward attendant to place me back on the bed. The room was spinning around me very quickly, and I was afraid I was going to fall off the bed. The oxygen was placed back on me. The nurse came into the room with the medication cup, containing a very small tablet. She removed the oxygen and told me to place the pill under my tongue. I pray to God I never have any of those experiences in my life again. It's like being by the ocean when everything is calm, and then suddenly a wave comes rushing in with full force. It keeps spreading until it reaches shore and ends with a very big splash.

As soon as the nurse placed the oxygen back on me and left the room, I began to feel something rushing from the pit of my stomach, spreading throughout my chest walls. I kept wondering what was happening to me. I had to try to relax and go with the flow, but this ride was not a pleasant one. It kept going like that until finally it reached up to my chest wall and then stopped. I realized I didn't need the oxygen anymore. I was able to breathe on my own. Shortly thereafter, the nurse walked into the room and removed the oxygen to check my pulse and respiration. She knew how long the glisphorine would take to put oxygen back into my heart, and that's why she immediately left the room.

Each and every day, I give thanks and praise to God for giving me another lease on life, but I pray that I don't ever have to go through that again. It was a very scary and unpleasant experience. Shortly after I was released from the hospital, I began having the same signs and symptoms as before. Meanwhile, I continued taking the pain medication, along with the aspirin. My physician was concerned and continued to monitor me closely. I felt helpless; it was a physical and emotional roller coaster for me. As time went on, the symptoms were still there. I had to deal with it and be a responsible parent.

I came across a small article in the newspaper saying that researchers found that extra virgin olive oil is the best oil to cook with, followed by canola oil. It further stated that it helps to fight and prevent infections. When I was through reading the newspaper, I found another article in a magazine that said a Japanese researcher and an American researcher found that extra virgin olive oil also helps to fight and prevent heart diseases and certain cancers, including breast and prostate cancer. As I sat there, the fly suddenly appeared on the article I was reading. I silently wondered if God was trying to tell me something in parables. I didn't know what to expect, for the fly only comes around when something bad is about to happen the following day. I silently asked God to protect me from whatever danger lay ahead of me, for I was still trying to overcome my near-death experience.

After reading the articles, I went to the supermarket and got the last gallon of Colavita extra virgin olive oil. I even said to myself, "Everybody is aware of the researchers' findings." When I returned home, I poured some of the oil into the olive oil bottle. I had been using the plain olive oil, knowing that's what we grew up on. Mom would cook our meals with it and even gave us a teaspoon to drink every day. When I was through pouring the oil, I had a glass of cranberry juice. As I sat there, the fly suddenly appeared on my hands again and then flew over me. I silently prayed I would have the strength and courage to handle whatever was about to be bestowed upon me again. That night on the news, including the world news, were the researchers' findings.

The following evening when I returned home, as soon as I took off my coat, I started with a slight cough before I could walk over to the stove to turn on the burner to make myself a cup of tea. I began to gasp for air. I couldn't breathe. The rest of my body felt fine, except for the pounding in my head as I continue to gasp for air. I looked at the phone and realized if I dialed 911, I would not have been able to give my address. At first I began to panic and then quickly realized from my training as a practical nurse, I had to remain calm. I then held in my breath as much as I could, hurriedly walk over to the kitchen cabinet, frantically opened the olive oil bottle, took one gulp, walked back as fast as I could, leaned against the kitchen wall, and waited for the final moment. In a split second after swallowing the extra virgin olive oil, I was able to breathe freely, without any respiratory complications. I was alive! I couldn't believe it! As I leaned against the wall, I thanked God for sparing my life again. I thought of the many people who suffer from asthma, including children. I wondered, *is this the way they feel?* This is seriously dangerous. I even thought of the firemen who risk their lives on a daily basis to help people. I wondered, *is this the way they feel from smoke inhalation?* This was indeed a serious, dangerous situation to be in. Every breath I tried to take in, the air was actually sucking up my lungs. I thanked God for giving me a new lease on life again and wondered if he was giving me a silent message.

When I got myself together, I called Mom and reminded her how much I love her. She wanted to know what was wrong, and I told her of my frightening experience. She advised me to see my physician as soon as possible. My daughter was spending the winter break with her. After reminding my daughter how much I love her and will always continue to love her, no matter what happens to me, she wanted to return home. I told her to continue spending the holidays with her grandmother and that I'd be all right. As I sat on the couch listening to songs of inspiration, Rovette, our dog, came and stood in front of me, wagging her tail. I hugged her and realized it was feeding time. After feeding her, we went out for a walk. I enjoyed the cool breeze on my face, thanking God once again for the gift of life.

Shortly thereafter, I saw my physician. I explained to her what had happened to me. After a thorough examination, everything was okay. She said maybe I was getting an asthma attack, coming in from the cold into the warmth. I let her know I never suffered from asthma. I continued to watch my diet. I was having mostly dark green, leafy vegetables tossed with extra virgin olive oil, along with salmon for lunch. I would have a glass of cranberry juice or a glass of vegetable juice, which included kale, spinach, broccoli, with lemon and lime, along with extra virgin olive oil. The signs and symptoms were still there as I continued on a physical roller coaster, hoping and praying to God that there would be an answer. I began observing that the medication was no longer helping the pain. I continued to be monitored closely by my physician on a regular basis. When I did see her again, I explained that the medication was not helping the pain; instead, the pain was getting worse. I even made a joke, telling her maybe the drug company is making a lot of money, that they are not putting all the ingredients into the medication. I asked her to give me a prescription for only one bottle, no more refills. Should I notice any change in regards to the pain-control substance, I would let her know.

There was still no improvement in my medical condition. However, at the end of the month, when I was through taking the medication, I was no longer having the signs and symptoms. I kept asking myself, *could this medication be the cause of my heart attack?* Or what I had been experiencing all along? I told my doctor about the change in my condition. I didn't want to be on any more pain-control substances. I held on, dealing with the pain the best way I knew how. I meditated, listened to songs of inspiration, and continued to watch what I ate. I found myself getting emotional often. I needed God to continue to help heal me. I took the time to admire the beautiful sky, the trees, the flowers, and wondered if God was too busy to know what I had been going through. Whenever I felt scared, I would hold the Bible close to my heart and cry out to God to heal my broken spirit. I have to admit, it helped me. I felt my life had changed somewhat. I no longer was interested in studying family law. I had already completed my studies academically, and I was content. Nothing of materialistic value was important to me. Rovette's love and her company, along with my daughter's love, my Mom, family, and friends helped me tremendously. It's truly a blessing to have the love of a dog around.

Two months after being off the medication, when I returned home and turned on the television, I could not believe what I was hearing. So many people had died from heart attacks while being on the said "pain-control substance." I became emotional. How could anyone, or even a drug company, risk human lives for a dollar and a buck? How could they? Do they know what it's like to have excruciating, explosive pain in your heart as your whole body shakes like an earth tremor? Do they know what it's like to see a very bright light, so bright it dazzles your eyesight? Are they aware of what it's like to be unable to see your child lying down on the bed as she recovers from a high temperature? Are they aware of what's it like to be very weak? And to find yourself sliding down off the chair? Are they aware of what it's like to find the physical and emotional strength to apply hard pressure to your own heart? Good God, have mercy! What on earth is the world coming to? Do you all at the drug company have a conscience? Would you like this to happen to your mother, wife, or children? Or even your own self, all because of the love of money? Someday we all will have to die, and we cannot take the money or anything else of materialistic value with us. How about our souls? Has it ever occurred to you that you will have to answer a higher power? What about the people who died innocently because they trusted you and your product to help them through their physical pain? Their spirits will haunt you until you have suffered the same fate as they have. Do you think you'll ever see the light? Much less enter into kingdom of heaven? Tell me something! What do you do when you all from the drug company look at yourselves in the mirror?

Do you rejoice and have a good laugh because you have conned so many of us into believing you? Do you think you can ever make up for the physical, traumatizing, psychological, post-traumatic, and emotional stress, you have caused so many families, including their children and grandchildren? How about you taking the same product you made for us unsuspecting victims? You wouldn't, would you? Because your life is too precious, while we the poor victims take it because we didn't know better. I can assure you, God will never let you get away with it. You might be on top of the world now, but sooner or later, God will show you and your company who's in charge. You all should be ashamed of yourselves for what you have put me and others through. Please do unto others as you would like them to do unto you and your family. Please, in God's name, start doing the right thing. Remember, there are over a million eyes watching you that you cannot see. If you don't do right by God and other human beings that are depending on you to help ease their physical pain, it will be only be a matter of time before he takes charge over you all. Please, it's not too late to start over again, to do the right thing. I don't think you want to keep testing God.

chapter 18

We had adopted Rovette; she was found in zero temperature. She was afraid not only of the cold, but also of human beings. The first day my daughter saw her, she fell in love with her. On her way from a daily walk with the trainer, she kept turning back to look at her. I knew she had chosen the right dog, but we were aware of the long road that was ahead of us. We could not have adopted her unless we met with her psychologist about how to treat her, knowing that she had been badly abused. Before we brought her home, we went shopping at the pet shop to ensure she had what she needed. My daughter even bought her cologne. We finally brought her home.

The first day she arrived home, after she was fed, my daughter took her out for a while. When they returned home, when my daughter was through washing her hands, she went into her room to watch a movie. I went in to let her know dinner was ready. As I sat down next to her, we heard a loud crashing sound. We looked at each other, wondering what was happening. When we came out, we found Rovette having herself a good meal. She had climbed up on the stove and threw down the pot with our dinner. Without a care in the world, she had herself a good feast. My daughter had a hearty laugh. I couldn't believe what I was seeing. When she was through eating, as she sat there, she just kept licking her lips and staring at me, letting me know in her silent way the dinner was good.

I had to let her know it was our dinner, not hers. I explained that this is now her home. We're here to protect her, not hurt her. There's no need to climb on the stove and eat our dinner, because our dinner is different from hers. We wanted her to trust us as much as we needed to trust her. She seemed to understand what I was saying. She just kept looking at me with her pretty brown eyes, silently letting me know it was "survival of the fittest for her." I have to admit, when I was through talking to her, I went into my room and cried. We had to settle for a sandwich. It took some time for me to keep reassuring her this was now her permanent home and we loved her. We never had the problem with her climbing up on the stove again.

With a lot of patience, tender care, and reassuring her, she finally settled in. One night, she finally began to bark. It took three months for her to bark, and when she did, we were overjoyed. We knew that she understood this was now her permanent home and not just temporary. She became our best friend. She seemed to understand whenever something was wrong. We enjoyed her being in our company, especially while we watched a movie. We wanted her to be close by at all times, except when we weren't at home. We never allowed her to go out in the cold without a special coat on, to make sure she felt safe.

One night I took her to the store with me and I couldn't take her inside. I tied her leash to the railing, reassuring her I would return shortly. A customer came into store to ask whose dog it was. I couldn't help laughing when she said she thought it was a human being sitting there, because of the pretty wool coat she had on. We made sure she had an egg crate mattress to sleep on at all times. It was indeed a pleasure to see how comfortably rested she was as she slept throughout the many nights.

Some of my friends complained that I was treating her like a human being. I had to let them know, a dog is truly a man's best friend and they make you feel very happy. The love you give to them, they give back to you. The only thing that they can't do is talk to you. They seem to understand what you say to them, as they wag their tail, jump on you when you least expect it, and kiss you in appreciation. We became protective of her, as much as she was protective of us, especially my daughter. She would lie at the front door and would not move until my daughter returned home. We had her for ten years. Unfortunately, recently she died of cancer. The vet told us we were lucky to have her for this long. It shows us what the power of love and affection can do, even for a helpless animal. She got it every step of the way, to the very end. We miss her a lot. We still get emotional talking about her. It will take us some time before we can adopt another dog.

chapter 19

As I write this chapter on this special day, Holy Thursday, the time is now 5:00 a.m. It's a very special time for me and my family as I reflect on God's wonderful love. I remember how Jesus died so viciously on the cross, among two thieves, for us sinners so that we can have a better life. I feel blessed to have been given another lease on life, to be with my family and friends. I'm here not by luck or by chance, but by a miracle.

I believe death can be a very frightening and traumatic experience when we are not prepared for it, especially when it's staring you in the face with no place to run or hide. Only a higher power holds our destiny in his hands; he decides how, where, and when we should die. I sincerely hope you can have and feel that inner peace that I've felt come over me when I felt I was ready to go over to the other side. However, when you're a parent, God gives us the physical strength and courage to fight for the love of the child that he has entrusted into our arms. God saw it was not his will to let me die at that time.

Shortly after the information was broadcasted on the news, I received a letter from the hospital informing me of the serious side effects of the product. I was further advised that records showed I had been on the medication, and they said I should stop taking it immediately. I was also asked to come in for further testing, another scary experience. One friend said I must have been doing something right in life to see a bright light. It may seem like a compliment, but I don't feel it is, not the explosive way it happened.

It's been a week for me to silently honor God in my way. I mostly listen to a prayer station to help me understand the teachings and more of the powerful word of God, along with the songs of inspiration. Without God, my life would be useless. His word is spiritual food for my soul. I sincerely hope you can also feel the same way about the most powerful, supernatural being of the universe.

Today my daughter has grown up into a beautiful young lady. She's attending college and is on the honor roll. She's also majoring in the medical field.

To those who are on prescription drugs, should you have any unusual signs or symptoms that you didn't have before you started taking the medication, please don't hesitate to consult your pharmacist. Follow his instructions and get in touch with your physician as soon as possible, or head for the nearest hospital. Please remember, time is crucial. Don't try to diagnose yourself. Make a note of how often you're having symptoms, what were you doing at the time they occurred, and how long they last. It is very important to relay the information to the doctor. This will help your physician diagnose the problem. Please remember, there are serious side effects to prescription drugs. Please do not take your health for granted.

To the parents who are doing two and three jobs to provide for your family, please take a moment for yourself and have a routine physical examination, including an EKG to be sure your heart is beating normally. Have blood tests to be certain you're not anemic or diabetic. Be sure everything else is normal externally and internally. You need to be sure all is well with your bones, or know how it should be treated. Ask your physician for a referral to see your ophthalmologist. Please insist he do a glaucoma test; this is one of the diseases that has no sign or symptoms. It can leave you permanently blind. Remember your gift of sight is one of the precious gifts that God has given us. Treasure it as you would your jewelry. Please always remember your children love and care for you very much. They may show it in different ways, but the most important thing to know is that they love and need you. Should anything bad happen to you, please remember their lives will never be the same without you.

Your life may not be what you want, but please try to be content and work toward what you really want to do to better yourself. You will have to make sacrifices. Don't let your children pressure you to buy what they want when you're working hard to make ends meet. Have a serious talk with your children and let them know the facts of life. Take the time to start loving and appreciating your body before it's too late. Please take care of your health. Be sure to include dark, leafy vegetables in your diet, especially kale. It takes a bit longer to cook, but it's worth it. Also include extra virgin olive oil in your meals. Look for the extra virgin olive oil that is green, not yellow. Please wash your dark, leafy vegetables thoroughly in white vinegar mixed with baking soda and lemon juice to help fight and prevent the bacteria that causes diseases. Include a dash of cinnamon in your meals. Please consult with your physician before using any of these products. Doing two and three jobs can be very stressful for your heart. You have to take very good care of yourself. Follow your gut instincts. Your intuition never leads you wrong.

To the young men and women, take your time and enjoy your life with self-discipline and self-control. Act in a responsible manner at all times. Appreciate your loved ones. Please don't be in a hurry to grow up; take your time. Always keep in mind it's most important to show love and appreciation to your mom each and every day. Don't ever leave home without a hug and a kiss good-bye, because at the end of the day, there's no guarantee you'll both see each other alive. Avoid taking her for granted. Don't let vanity go to your head because your friends think you're all that. Remember in times of trouble or sickness, you cannot always count on your friends to be there for you. What goes around will certainly come around. Maybe someday you'll have a child, and the way you treated your mom, your child will end up treating you the same way. By then, she may not be around anymore. There won't be any turning back to say to her, "Mom, I'm sorry for the way I've treated you." She's your mom at all times, not your slave. Don't treat her like one. And please always keep in mind there's a higher power above watching your every move. Whatever you do, don't let materialistic things be a main factor in your life. Don't ever demand that your parents, especially your mom, buy expensive clothes for you when she can barely put food on the table. Keep in mind, it's not the clothes on your back that are important; it's what's in your heart. The inner beauty shines from both inside and out. Avoid trying to impress anyone. A true friend will like you as you are.

You'll never know how lucky each and every one of you are to be born and living in one of the greatest countries in the world. You have free high school education, free books, transportation, lunch, freedom of speech, and the rest that follows. All you need to do is apply yourselves, starting with self-discipline and self-control. It's very important to have a good education. If you're having trouble reading or with any other subjects, don't feel ashamed or embarrassed to ask for help. Turn to your guidance counselors; they certainly can help you. Or you can even go to the library. There are tutors there who will help you succeed in whatever subjects you're having problems with.

Please don't deny yourself the right to a good education, which you're worthy of having. If you don't seize the opportunity to have an education, you'll be cheating yourself. Your education will never go out of style; it will always be there. Focus positively on what you want to do in your life from now on. Don't talk about it. Make a list of what you want to positively accomplish in your life. Place it near the bathroom mirror, your bedroom, or even on the refrigerator door. Include your mom in your plans. Let her continue to be proud of you, and avoid bringing her to her knees in tears. Do the right things in life. You'll be amazed at the tremendous blessings God will shower you with. It may not happen right away or overnight, but it will definitely happen. Trust in God and include him in your plans. Please, always remember everything good takes hard work, patience, determination, perseverance, and endurance. There will be stumbling blocks along the way. That's okay. Get up, dust yourself off, and call on God to guide you along your way to your successful endeavor. Please keep him in your mind and in your heart at all times. Remember, Jesus, the son of the living most high, was beaten, tortured, and died on the cross to give us a better life, and he has the power to take it away from us. Be a leader in a positive way at all times, not a follower. Be proud of yourself, and remember you are a special blessing from God the most high. Each and every one of us has a calling in life. Take the time to communicate with your God. He'll help you find your true calling. Before you begin to grumble or complain about anything, thank him for your many blessings. Always remember, tomorrow is not ours. Life is very precious, yet so short. God controls our destiny at all times, not man. Reach out to him and talk to him. He wants you to reach out to him. If you take a moment to turn off the television, the phone, or whatever you might be doing, and focus on him for a few minutes, you may be able to feel him close to your heart. Take the time to read the Bible and understand how great and powerful he is. Keep in mind he's a loving and forgiving God. Don't wait until you find yourself in trouble with the law and then call on him to help you, when you don't even thank him for the roof over your head or the bed you sleep on. Before you leave home to hang out with the wrong crowd, keep repeating these words to yourself: "I will not let a few minutes of committing an illegal activity destroy my life, my parents' lives, or the intended victim and his family's lives forever." Please let these words continue to be your motto in life. Don't hurt or kill another human being and then feel sorry tomorrow. It'll make no sense. By then, it will be too late. Avoid the excuse of not having a role model or a male figure in your life. It's hogwash. With God on your side, you can accomplish anything positive you set your mind to do. Follow your heart's desire. Act on it now. No more excuses. You are a blessed child of God, with the precious gift of life, which he has given to you. You don't have to prove anything to your friends—just to your mom and those who believe in you.

Be kind and courteous at all times, especially to your elders. Take the time to visit a sick child whose life is not guaranteed for tomorrow. Visit the individuals who are deaf, dumb, or blind in an institution. Give them words of inspiration, even if it's to one person. You can help inspire and motivate them more than you'll ever know. You will see how the less fortunate live in a world of their own, and yet they are content because they have peace and God in their lives. I'm sure they will certainly help to inspire and motivate you as well. Please have your parent or guardian accompany you to those places, and remember to brace yourself because it will be emotional. Hopefully the experience will help you to face the reality of how truly blessed you are. Sometimes in life, we may only have a split second to make a decision that can change our life forever. Let your decision be a positive one at all times.

To the daughter-in-laws: Before you got married, you did everything in your power to impress your intended mother-in-law! Nevertheless, she had concerns that you were not the right one to make her son happy. You were determined to convince her you were the right one.

Once you got married, you began to turn your nose up at your mother-in-law, calling her all sorts of names in the book. Telling your husband when he can and cannot see his own mother, even giving him orders that you don't want her in your home anymore. Meanwhile, he's afraid to call his own mother. Your husband is not yours to order around like a puppy dog. His mother is the woman that chose to bring her child into the world. God has only entrusted your husband to you to love, respect, adore, cherish, and for you both to take very good care of each other—not to be taken for granted. He only leased him to you, as he leases us our lives. At any given day, when he steps out the door, you may never see him again. God has a way of teaching us a lesson when we think we have gotten too big for our shoes. Please treat your mother-in-law with the respect she deserves. We sometimes think the mother-in-law wants to keep her son for herself, and doesn't want him to get married, or she doesn't want to let him go. Put yourself in her place. Appreciate his mom for the wonderful job she did in raising her child. Do not deprive your children of the love from their grandparents. You don't need any regrets. May God help you to find love, peace, and unity in your heart toward your husband's mother. Let peace continue to reign in your home, before it's too late. In appreciation for her son, give your mother-in-law a call. Please remember, there's no guarantee we'll see tomorrow. May God continue to bless and keep you and your family safe in his loving arms.

To the son-in laws: Your wife didn't fall from an apple tree straight into your arms. Her mother carried her under her heart for nine months. When her heart beat, so did her child's heart. She did everything in her power to ensure all went with her until she met you. Your wife is not your personal property. She's your wife to love, cherish, adore, and respect at all times. God has only leased her to you, as he leases us our lives. If you don't do right by your wife and the mother that brought her child into this world, God will certainly show you who is in control of your destiny. Please respect your mother-in-law at all times. Treat her as you would your mama. Had she not raised her daughter in a respectable manner, you would not have given her a second look.

To parents: Please protect your children. Let them be your top priority. Don't put anyone else before them. Always remember, people will come and go in your lives, but your children may be the ones who are there for you throughout the end, depending on how you treat them. You will not remain young and beautiful forever. They need you now to love and protect and guide them. Someday, they will definitely thank you for taking very good care of them.

Avoid allowing your children to go out and play by themselves. Please take the time to accompany them at all times. Hold their hands, even if you think they'll slip away. Please remember, our children are not ours to have and to hold. God has only entrusted them into our loving arms to love, nurture, and care for, and depending on how we treat them, he has the final word. Try to protect your children at all times and continue to keep God in your heart.

To the fathers who have neglected their children: You cannot see the void in their hearts or the emotional anguish on their faces, thinking maybe, just maybe, today may be the day they'll see you. Please keep in mind, our children are not ours to have and to hold, mistreat or abuse for our own selfish purpose. God wants us to love and protect his precious, innocent children! We are all his children, but where the minor children are concerned, he take's that very personally. He has entrusted them into our care, because he loves and trusts us. As a father, you are going down in age, and the child or children you have neglected, may someday be the ones to give you a glass of water to help save your life. Your children need you now to help them to be emotionally and spiritually strong. Give them the love, security, and stability that every child needs to become productive members of society. Emphasize to them the importance of having a good education. Please, it's imperative that your child continue to see their pediatrician until they are seventeen years old. You may find it's a lot of trouble to keep your child's appointment, but please remember the love and care you give your children today will certainly come back to you tomorrow. Regardless of how busy you are, find the time to pay close attention to your child's needs. They are the future leaders of tomorrow. Meanwhile, you have to be the voice for them when they cannot speak for themselves. Build up your children's self-esteem, especially if they had a rough day at school. Pay close attention to your children. You don't have to be a doctor or a nurse to know if there's anything physically wrong with them. Look at their facial expression, the pupil of their eyes. As a parent, you can determine if they are yellow or pale. Look at their body language; it can tell you a story. One day, your children will thank you for being protective of them, and in turn, they will become very protective of you, as I was of my mom.

Please don't leave the responsibilities of a parent to the maid. Someday the love that your child was supposed to give to you as a parent will be given to the maid instead. Don't let the stranger that helps you cross the street when you suddenly have blurred vision turn out to be the son or daughter you abandoned as a child. Don't let your attending physician that stands at your bedside to give you the bad news of your health turn out to be the son you abandoned when his mother told you she was pregnant, all because you didn't want that kind of responsibility. In heaven's name, please do the right thing, because God has a way of making the impossible become the possible when we least expect it. Avoid putting your children through the emotional and psychological turmoil of not being in their lives. Wherever you are, whatever you are doing, try your best to reach out to your children. Don't let them continue to walk around blaming themselves for you not wanting to be in their lives. Tomorrow may be too late. God will give you the strength and courage to help you to be the best dad you can be.

To the young mothers: Please remember your body is a temple. Try your best to have self-respect and self-control. Being a parent, it's your responsibility to help protect your child. Let your children be the top priority in your life. Protect them in every way you possibly can. Take the time to continue to show them love, affection, and attention. Remember you are their role model and they are looking up to you for guidance. Help steer them in the right direction. You have a tough job ahead of you, but you can do it. Please avoid taking out your frustration on them, and remember they didn't ask to come into this world. They are a precious gift to you from God with love. Always be loving and kind to them. Should you feel tired or frustrated, take a minute and splash some cold water on your face until you feel refreshed. Walk back into the room, hold your children close to your heart, and remind them how much you love them. Make them feel loved and secure, and not scared of you because "Mommy is angry." Please don't be mean to your children. Please avoid having Tom, Dick, and Harry babysit your children. If possible, take them with you wherever you go. Don't ever leave them home alone. Have a close relative or trusted friend babysit. It's very important to have your child grow up in a safe and loving environment. It's imperative for you to have a thermometer at home at all times. It's very important to know the normal body temperature and the normal pulse. As a parent, from my personal experience, it's crucial to know these things. In case of an emergency, it can help you know what to do to help save your child's life. I recommend that you take a certified course in CPR and First Aid. The Red Cross and other organizations offer those courses for a small fee. I'm certain you can make the sacrifice to do so. I believe the hairdresser or the dress department can wait until you have paid for the courses. Please, do this for the love of your children. Don't take their lives for granted. Always be prepared. A lot can happen in the split of a second, when you least expect it. You don't need to hear the words of, "if only had you done this, your child would probably be alive." Please do the right thing, and you'll certainly be rewarded by the grace of God.

To the men and women who have already lost their eyesight: Take heed, and don't feel scared or discouraged. Be of good cheer. Remember God will not forsake or leave you alone in times of trouble. Try to remain as calm as you possibly can. Try not to panic. When you feel scared and alone, hold your Bible close to your heart, and cry out to God to give you the strength and courage to help you face another new day. Continue to visit your ophthalmologist and physician for routine examinations. Please try to have a loved one accompany you to and from your examinations. Even if you are physically challenged, the Brooklyn Center for Individuals with Disability (BCID) will help guide you every step of the way. A few of their employees are also physically challenged and will certainly understand what you're going through physically and emotionally. They will give you the emotional support that you'll need to help you face the most challenging experiences of your life. Their telephone number is 718–998–4659.

They are professionals there who can help you deal with your loss. Your life may not be the same. The friends you may have had before you became blind or disabled may slowly disappear, and it's not that they don't care—maybe it's because emotionally they cannot handle the fact that you are blind or maybe losing your sight, knowing at one time you were the life of the party. Emotionally you'll be hurting, but please don't despair. You'll meet new friends. Try your very best not to be out alone at all times. Remember you are now in a vulnerable position, and you don't want to become an easy target.

You'll have to learn to read braille. Always remember, when we lose one sense, the other senses tend to get sharper. You'll find yourself being more alert to everything. Don't forget to have your loved one inquire about the Gift of Sight program. Please remember, everything may not move as fast as you would like, but with faith, patience, prayers, and determination, everything's going to be all right. God will always be standing at your side. Continue to reach out to him. There are times you'll be angry and upset; it's understandable, but it will do you no good. It'll only make you feel sick to your stomach and may cause further medical complications or even slow down your recovery. If you have never needed God before, you'll definitely need him now, more than ever. Keep the faith, and remember don't ever give up hope. Prayers can move stubborn mountains.

chapter 20

Wwe as human beings, living on God's green pasture here on earth, will have problems. It's up to us to know how to handle the problem. Sometimes, when we think we have it tough, all we have to do is take the time to look around us. The homeless people that sleep on the cold pavement because they have nowhere to live feel safer there than in a shelter. Sometimes, my heart bleeds for these people. How did they find themselves in that position? Offering them a hot meal may soothe their souls a bit, just knowing another human being cares. You can help make a difference. The fact is, sometimes in life, circumstances can throw us into many different directions.

Take the time to give the homeless words of inspiration; it will help them realize they are special in the eyes of God. He hasn't forgotten them. They are his children, regardless of their circumstances in life, because he has created them. There is a higher power above who watches over us and will continue to guide and protect us, even open a way for us when there seems to be little hope. All we have to do is hold onto God's unchanging love, and he'll see us through. It may not happen overnight, but he will certainly come through for us when we least expect it. The rest of our problems will fall into place. Remember the story where it took God forty years to free the people of Israel. All we have to do is keep the faith and never, ever give up hope.

To the bartenders and managers of a bar: You should be held

accountable for serving over-the-limit drinks to your customers. Your customer may have a problem with his children being on drugs, a foreclosure on his home, or other problems that he cannot handle. He comes into your bar and talks about his problems to you. Say, "Excuse me, sir, you've had enough to drink," instead of continuing to sell him alcohol. Don't just be interested in how much money and tips you collect from this one customer. Once he gets behind the wheel, he's not only putting his life in danger, but also the lives of innocent human beings, which could be your wife, mother, daughter, or grandmother that he kills. Some customers feel on top of the world talking to the bartender about his or her problem. To the vulnerable customers, the bartender is like a therapist.

To those who may be having a celebration at their home, before you invite your guests, be aware how many people will be attending and how much alcohol you'll be serving. Please act in a responsible and caring manner toward your guests. Please avoid letting your guests drive home under the influence of alcohol. Call a cab for each one of your guests, or allow them to remain overnight at your home, to sleep it off. Please ensure your guests are over twenty-one if they're going to drink alcohol.

Shortly after Mom's death, I tried to continue writing from where I left off. It was very difficult for me. I needed to hear a particular song to help motivate me. I began scanning through radio stations and came across a song with a reggae rhythm combined with an African beat. It sounded beautiful. When the artist began to sing, the words to his song were very positive. As I continued to listen to the song, I realized this was what I needed to hear to help motivate me. I needed to know who the artist was. I learned he was a very popular African artist who was loved around the world for his positive messages, which is of peace from his personal experiences. Shortly after he was through singing, the DJ said he was killed in the presence of his children in an attempted carjacking. It was a very solemn night, as the listeners kept calling in to offer their condolences to his family. At the time, the radio station was celebrating its fifth year anniversary being on the air. They kept on playing his beautiful music throughout the night. Maybe, just maybe, Mom's spirit wanted me to listen to his music to help motivate me to continue to type.

I believe there's life after death. I often wonder why bad things happen to good people. Only God has the answer. Maybe he's testing our faith. Regardless of what you may be going through or how tough life may seem, please remember there's a light beyond the tunnel. Find a special time to kneel down and pray with your children. Instill God in their lives at an early age, letting them know there's a higher power above who created them and the world. Please try and keep a Bible at home at all times. Teach them to pray for other children around the world.

Try to find the time to volunteer serving meals to the homeless at the shelter. It can be on any day of the week. Give a few words of inspiration to the heartbroken men and women at the shelter. Just a smile and a few words from you can help lift the broken at heart. In return, you'll feel richly blessed. If possible, try to volunteer at least once a week; this may help to empower your life. Instead of complaining, you may get to experience what's it like for the homeless not to have their own beds to sleep on or not to have a decent shower.

Mom would tell us, whatever we do, to always call on Jesus. There will be stumbling blocks along the way, but just hold and call on him to take the lead in your life. He'll help you remove whatever stumbling blocks may be standing in the way for you and your family. Once you put him first in your life, you'll see the remarkable change in your life and in your home. You may not want to believe it's possible, but I can assure you that with him, all things are possible. With God in our life, in our heart, and in our soul, we can overcome any obstacle. Please just take a moment to ask him to come into your life.

chapter 21

Two years ago when my daughter was through using the computer, she asked me if there was anyone I would like to search for. I told her I would like to see if my friend is living in New York. I told her who he was and how we met. At the time, she only had twenty-four hours to use the service. Surprisingly, only his name showed up with an address. I was still grieving over Mom's death and was in the midst of my writing, which was very emotional for me. I just wanted to remain focused. I figured when I was through writing, I'd get in touch with him. Besides, he was unaware I'd been residing in New York. When I finally completed the book, I asked my daughter to check another website to see if there wasn't another address. His name did appear with both addresses. After talking to my friend Michael about Rashid, I needed his advice about what I should do. He advised me I should meet with him and find closure. He also said, "You never know, you both might grow old together." I told him I wasn't sure about that. Anyhow, he told me when I was ready to let him know and he'd take me to see him.

I did a background check on him and found out that he was a bachelor without any criminal record. Had I found out he was married, I wouldn't have let him know I was residing in New York. I certainly didn't want to interrupt his life. Before leaving home, I wrote a letter reminding him who I was and how we met. Had he not been there, I would have slipped it under the door.

The day finally arrived. I confided in Michael that I was ready to see him again. I was very apprehensive. When we arrived at his home, Michael said to me, "Here we are. This is the address." I replied, "Oh God, I can't do this." He said to me, "You have come a long way. You can't turn back now." He then asked, "Would you like me to check for you," and I said yes.

As I sat nervously in the car, I looked back to see what was happening. He stood speaking to someone. I then saw the reflection of a tall figure standing at the side of the door. When he looked outside toward the car, I immediately recognized him. They both walked toward the car. Rashid had his hands in his pockets. I watched his every move. When he finally reached the car, he slightly bent forward. I put down the window and greeted him. "Hi, Rashid." He remembered me right away. It took me several minutes before I found the courage to get out and greet him face-to-face. We embraced. We finally found each other again not two years after seeing each other, but forty years later. Right here in New York City. It can only happen in New York. After introducing Michael to Rashid, he realized we had a lot of catching up to do. He told me when I was ready to leave, to call him. We were reunited five days before his birthday. We could not believe how time had passed. There was no need to slip the letter under the door. I personally gave it to him. My daughter couldn't believe we found each other again, and not in Trinidad, but in New York. God has given me another lease on life and a second chance to be with my first love.

It couldn't be a much happier time for us. God bless the day my daughter asked me if there was anybody I wanted to search for. Otherwise, I would not have thought to search for him, due to the emotional pain I was still going through after the death of Mom. Michael called later on to find out if I was ready to return home. Rashid said he would take me home instead. Before returning home, we went out for dinner to celebrate our reunion.

Rashid has stood by my side throughout the good and the bad times. Through it all, he's still the gentleman who has class, integrity, and dignity. He's still a warm, loving, caring, and kindhearted person, who is very considerate and shows compassion toward his family and his friends in need. We take the time to appreciate each other as often as we possibly can. We don't take anything in our lives for granted. Instead, we feel richly blessed to talk to each other on a daily basis and continue a new chapter in our lives. Hopefully God will continue to bless and keep us safe as we try our best to continue from where we left off, walking in faith and not by sight.

My friend Agnes was supposed to come to New York to celebrate our reunion. Unfortunately, it wasn't meant to be. God had a much bigger plan in store for her. Agnes and I came from loving families that instilled tough love to ensure we walked the straight and narrow path in life. We grew up together and attended the same school. When she left elementary school to attend a private high school, I missed her terribly. She was not only my best friend, she was like a sister to me. She also used to help protect me from the bullies at school. During my training as a telecommunications operator, whenever she worked the night shift she would take me under her wing and show me the different extension to the medical wards and other departments, just in case I was assigned to the hospital. When I completed my training, my first assignment was to work at the General Hospital.

Even though we lived across the ocean, we always found the time from our busy schedule to communicate with each other. I always found the time to thank her for showing me how to use the different extensions so that I was able to master the switchboard. With a lot of practice, I did just fine. Recently, we were making plans for us to be reunited in New York with Rashid. She was very happy to know we had finally been reunited after all those years. The following week after we spoke, I received a call at 7:00 a.m. informing me that she died at 4:00 a.m. I felt heartbroken. We hadn't seen each other in a few years, and there we were making plans to celebrate a special occasion. We had absolutely no idea that while we were making our own plans, God had a much bigger plan in store for her.

My daughter and I went to Trinidad to attend my best friend's funeral. It was the first time my daughter had the opportunity to see where I was originally born and raised. I was upset because this was not how it was supposed to be. I was not supposed to attend her funeral. We were supposed to spend some time together. God holds our destiny in the palm of his hands. The service was held at the same church where I attended services while growing up across the river. It was where I sang in the choir, made my First Communion, had my Confirmation, and where I would run to hide from the bullies. The ceremony was beautiful. Oh! How I wished she didn't have to die, but God was in control of the situation.

The school opposite to the church is still standing, and the boys' school is still downstairs. There have been a lot of changes to the school, and also in the district where I grew up. The bridge is still standing strong over the river. I had the opportunity to look around the house I grew up in. There are now three houses located over there. At my cousin's home, I was taken aback by the beautiful lilies that Lenny had loved, which were placed at the center of the table. At the back of the house were the coconut trees, the limes, mangoes, and also the beautiful flowers in the garden, which reminded me of the way I grew up! What was ironic was that nine years ago on that day, I suffered a heart attack along with a near-death experience. It was also my cousin's birthday. We started off the morning in prayer, thanking God for giving me another lease on life having the chance to be at home to celebrate her birthday and also to see my best friend laid to rest. It was unbelievable. What an experience it was. Agnes was buried in the same cemetery as Lenny. Their graves are not far from each other. It was heart wrenching to see her coffin being lowered into the ground. How can we ever overcome the death of a loved one? I don't think we ever can, but with time, I believe the emotional pain will get a little easier.

I had the privilege of meeting my ex-coworkers from the hospital, and also some from the inn. I learned my friend, the maître de at the inn, died last year, along with a few other workers. I felt very sad to know this, but I realize it's all part of life.

Before Agnes died, she was promoted to telephone operating supervisor. She was married and blessed with one biological child. She adopted three other children, including a blind young girl, who's happily married. She'll always be remembered as a warm, loving, kindhearted person with a bubbly personality. She knew how to cheer you up when the chips were down. She loved helping others, especially those who were less fortunate. When we last spoke, she told me of her wedding anniversary that was coming up, and reminded me that I had introduced her to the most loving, caring person, whom she had been happily married to. She would say to me that I had to be there for her special occasion. Unfortunately, it was not meant to be. Her work on earth is over, but her job in heaven has just begun. I have to admit, I miss talking to her very much. With the help of God and the emotional support from my family and friends, including Rashid, I'll be okay. February 28 was her birthday, and February 29 was her wedding anniversary. Sadly, she didn't live to see either. I'm sure she's in heaven rejoicing along with Mom, Lenny, Dad, her parents, and the archangels watching down from the golden gates of heaven.

Winding down to the end of my book, it became very emotional for me to continue. As I began to scan through the radio, there were spiritual hymns playing on a station, and I realized that was what I needed—spiritual food for my soul. It was the first day the station was on the air. After I attended one of their concerts, I discussed with my brother how beautiful the concert was and told him I had the pleasure of meeting the manager of the station. I was taken aback when my brother said to me, "He's my good friend." Shortly thereafter, I had a dream where Mom showed me a church that was lit very bright, and she said to me, "This is the church, and the radio station is inside of the church." I had absolutely no idea what she was talking about. I met with one of the reverends at the church and was surprised when I saw the same color of the church and the same bright lights as I saw in my dream. On the said night, having seen the manager and his wife, during our conversation, they were surprised to learn who my brother was. I mentioned the dream I had the previous night and what Mom had said to me, and there I was standing inside the church that I saw in my dream. I was unaware he had attended Mom's funeral. Today, my brother is on the air. Now I understand what she was trying to tell me in parables—that my brother Mitch would be working at the radio station. I guess Mom is in the right place in heaven beside God and can see what will happen to us in the future. I believe Mom's spirit will continue to smile down on us and everyone else's lives she has touched in one way or another.

As I reflect back, I remember when I was told I had to prove my mother was my biological mother. It brought me to tears. She was the only person I knew who loved, guided, and protected me throughout my life. It was imperative for me that she prove she was indeed my Mom. I felt humiliated. I looked at Mom and wondered if it was worth going through the humiliation of proving she was indeed my biological mother. At that moment, I felt deep within my heart, mind, body, soul, and spirit that she was indeed worth fighting for with every ounce of my being in order to prove she was indeed my biological mother. Mom will always be remembered for the love and attention she gave to her children, protecting us and ensuring our safety at all times. She instilled God in our lives at an early age, and with tough love she made sure we walked the straight and narrow path in life. In return, we loved and protected her. She made the ultimate sacrifice to sponsor her children, ensuring they are all American citizens. I know she's looking down at us from the golden gates of heaven, along with Lenny, Dad, my best friends, along with God and his archangels, shielding and helping to protect us from whatever dangers they see that maybe lurking around the corner.

Ma, I have finally completed this book in your honor. It was nine years ago that I started to write this in order to honor you. Unfortunately, due to circumstances beyond my control, I almost didn't make it. As I reflect back, it also took you nine years of going back and forth for me to see the top specialist, but you didn't give up on me. We finally made it. It was seven years later, after he did the surgery on me, he humbly apologized to you for the humiliation you went through to see him. I thank you, Mom, for your love and guidance and for protecting me in every way possible. You'll never know how safe and secure you made me feel knowing I could hear your every word, smell the beautiful perfume you wore, and feel your gentle touch on my forehead as you prayed over me while I lay floating in a hole of darkness. Knowing you were always close by, letting me know your every movement, my stage level continued to improve. Throughout the years, I have tried my very best to make you proud of me, Mom, as much as I have always been proud of you and continue to worship you. I often wondered how you got the strength and tremendous courage to deal with the physical and emotional suffering of Lenny's death, especially without Dad at your side. The many days you stood alone in the rain to ensure the cocoa was put away and that we were safely inside as you continued to plant the vegetables in the pouring rain. I prayed that the day would come when you didn't have to do that anymore. It took some time, but it eventually happened. Thank you, Ma, for your patience and endurance. You'll never know how safe you made me feel when you held my hand and walked me back into the school to meet with the principal. Oh, how I wanted to tell you so many times of the beatings I received at the hands of the bullies, especially the blows at the back of my head. Even though you suspected something was wrong with me, I kept denying it. I was too scared to say a word. From the day you found out, you made me feel brave and emotionally strong so that I could handle anything life throws at me. You made sure you were there to meet and greet Mitch and me after school, watching and observing everyone's movement around us as we walked home. I never anticipated for one moment that when I dedicated that special song for you on Mother's Day it would be the last Mother's Day you would live to be with us.

A very special thank you, Mom, for your unconditional love. Please forgive me if I shed a few tears. It has been a long and emotional journey for me to get to this final stage. Please continue to rest in peace. I'll love and cherish you in my heart forever and ever, until we meet on the other side. May God and his archangels continue to guide and protect you. May your soul always rest in peace with love from your other loving children and me forever and ever. Amen!